D1056327

The Practitioner Inquiry Series
Marilyn Cochran-Smith and Susan L. Lytle, *SERIES EDITORS*

(continued)

Immigrant Students and Literacy

READING, WRITING, AND REMEMBERING

Gerald Campano

Foreword by Sonia Nieto

TEACHERS COLLEGE PRESS

TEACHERS COLLEGE | COLUMBIA UNIVERSITY

NEW YORK AND LONDON

Published by Teachers College Press, 1234 Amsterdam Avenue, New York, NY 10027

Portions of Chapter 3 are reprinted from "The Second Class: Providing Space in the Margins," by G. Campano, 2005, *Language Arts, 82*, pp. 186–194. Copyright 2005 by the National Council of Teachers of English. Reprinted with permission.

Portions of Chapter 5 are adapted from "Ma-Lee's Story," by G. Campano, in *Going Public with Our Teaching: An Anthology of Practice* (pp. 237–242), edited by T. Hatch et al., 2002, New York: Teachers College Press. Copyright 2005 by Teachers College Press. Adapted with permission.

Portions of Chapter 7 are reprinted from "Performing Identities Through Drama and Teatro Practices in Multilingual Classrooms," by C. Medina and G. Campano, 2006, *Language Arts, 83*, pp. 332–341. Copyright 2005 by the National Council of Teachers of English. Reprinted with permission.

Library of Congress Cataloging-in-Publication Data

Campano, Gerald.
    Immigrant students and literacy : reading, writing, and remembering / Gerald Campano ; foreword by Sonia Nieto.
        p.   cm.—(Practitioner inquiry series)
    Includes bibliographical references and index.
    ISBN-10: 0-8077-4732-7 (pbk. : alk. paper)
    ISBN-10: 0-8077-4733-5 (cloth alk. paper)
    ISBN-13: 978-0-8077-4732-2 (pbk. alk. paper)
    ISBN-13: 978-0-8077-4733-9 (cloth : alk. paper)
    1. Children of immigrants—Education—United States.   2. Multicultural education—United States.   3. Language arts—United States.   I. Title.

    LC3746.C36 2007
    371.826'9120973—dc22   2006021629

ISBN-13:   ISBN-10:
978-0-8077-4732-2 (paper)   0-8077-4732-7 (paper)
978-0-8077-4733-9 (cloth)   0-8077-4733-5 (cloth)

Printed on acid-free paper
Manufactured in the United States of America

20   19   18   8

If you want to know what we are, look upon the farms or upon the hard pavement of the city. You usually see us working or waiting for work, and you think you know us, but our outward guise is more deceptive than our history.

Our history has many strands of fear and hope, that snarl and converge at several points in time and space. We clear the forest and the mountains of the land. We cross the river and the wind. We harness wild beast and living steel. We celebrate labor, wisdom, peace of the soul.

—Carlos Bulosan, *Freedom from Want*

Contents

Foreword

BEING A TEACHER TODAY is no easy matter. Increasing demands on teachers, including larger classes, pressures to follow a rigid standardized curriculum and "teach to the test," and decreased support for public education, result in pressure cooker schools that are unengaging for both teachers and students. Sadly, many teachers fall victim to the challenges of teaching, especially new teachers in urban schools, about half of whom leave the profession within five years. It is clear, then, that teaching takes tremendous commitment, enormous energy, and a good measure of talent. Given this reality, why would people choose teaching as a career, particularly in urban settings with students of diverse racial and linguistic backgrounds, many of whom live in poverty?

Gerald Campano's response to this question is a moving antidote to the disheartening and discouraging reality of public education today. Written as a series of "critical stories" of classroom life, IMMIGRANT STUDENTS AND LITERACY is a moving portrayal of his work as a fifth-grade teacher in an urban classroom with immigrant children of various backgrounds. Through an array of literacy strategies that tap into students' cultural traditions and life experiences, Campano illustrates what it takes to be a teacher with heart and soul, not simply one who succumbs to the increasing calls for higher test scores and standardized curricula.

There are many lessons to be learned from this gem of a book. For one, Campano's notion of a "second classroom" where teachers interact with, and nurture, students outside official classroom time is a reminder that teaching goes on all the time whether teachers intend for it to happen or not. Teachers' attention—or lack of it—to students' backgrounds, interests, and experiences says a great deal of what they think about their students and how they care for them, or not. This "second classroom," as Campano defines it, is both a pedagogical and an ideological space, a space neither visible nor compensated through official channels, yet as important, or even more important, than the goings-on of the "first classroom."

A second lesson that resonates throughout this book is the need to be skeptical of conventional wisdom concerning immigrant students. If teaching is, as Campano maintains, an "ethical practice," then teachers need to be wary of negative labels and expectations based on students' race/ethnicity, gender, or social position. Contrary to the expectations of many, Campano's students are intelligent young people and prolific writers who know their hearts and minds and who have great hopes for their futures in spite of the circumstances of their present realities. This point is made vividly clear in the book through the student-written and -performed play "What the Teacher Didn't Know," where classroom vignettes are frozen to provide insights into the lives of immigrant youths. Professional development, in this way, becomes a way of forging relationships with students who might otherwise be silenced and invisible in their dealings with teachers. In this way, professional development becomes not a static activity but instead an active and ever-changing pursuit.

A third lesson of this powerful book is the need to rethink curriculum to include children's lives, not just as antiseptic, unrelated material to add as "ethnic content," but rather as the very fabric of what goes on in classrooms. The children tell compelling survival stories based on their families' experiences of immigration, poverty, and oppression. Whether it is Celso's story of his grandfather's memory box or Carmen's account of caring for her dying father, these reflections are both food for thought and grist for the curriculum, and Campano uses them in sensitive and thoughtful ways to create a vibrant, diverse, and strong classroom community.

IMMIGRANT STUDENTS AND LITERACY is not a "feel-good" book. Insensitive bureaucracies and uncaring educators result in few happy endings. As Campano follows his students for several years through their academic experiences, he finds that too many of them fall through the cracks after they leave his classroom. Nevertheless, this is also a book filled with joy, one that reverberates with children's dreams of a better future. If teachers and other educators heed Campano's message that teaching and learning are most of all about relationships, we can indeed be hopeful about the education of immigrant students in the years to come

—Sonia Nieto

Preface

THE DETAILS OF MY GRANDFATHER'S LIFE are vague, even to his immediate family. He was born in 1910 on the northern coast of Mindanao; his people were poor farmers. "The only food we had," he recalled in an interview I conducted with him, "was what we could grow in our backyard." Orphaned around the age of 12, my grandfather lived with his older sister, but eventually made his way to Manila in search of employment opportunities to support his relatives. For a period he was one of Manila's street children. He eventually met an American teacher who told him of an opportunity to work for the United States Navy even though he did not meet the mandated age requirements. My grandfather considered this the first in a number of fortuitous encounters with individuals who helped him overcome obstacles to his passage to the United States. As my grandmother, his wife of 60 years, once told me, "He always found people; he always found a community."

The vessel he was assigned to was destined for the docks of San Pedro, California. Like other Filipino migrants from his generation, my grandfather left his colonized country in search of a better life. During the voyage he may have also learned a lesson about how individuals become marked as inferior because they are foreign. He told me that some of the sailors on the boat did not call him by his name, Faustino. Instead they referred to him as Friday, based on the "native servant" character in Defoe's *Robinson Crusoe*. The sailors engaged in what Werner Sollors (1990) labels "boundary-supporting" verbal strategies, which have the effect of distancing people so that they appear "childlike" and "primitive" (p. 299). More than simple insensitivity, this act of naming carried with it the intention to subordinate the ethnic "other" into a second-class status.

However, unlike the Friday of *Robinson Crusoe*, who remained stranded in servitude, my grandfather did not acquiesce to the name or its attendant social ascription. He refused to be called Friday and instead decided to go by the name of Freddy. He also told me he continued to try to "get along with everyone" and even achieved solidarity with his fellow sailors and stewards, Filipino and non-Filipino alike.

This strategic act of renaming and self-definition was perhaps my grandfather's "Faustian bargain," a way he could resist the negative stereotype of Friday while at the same time adapting to overcome isolation. If survival meant adopting a new name and working as a servant or houseboy, so be it. These roles may have made claims on his identity, but not monolithic claims. He would perform the work necessary to procuring invaluable resources for himself and his family. And as he also suggested to me, he continued to (re)evaluate his past experiences: "At the time I didn't like Faustino, but now I realize Faustino is a classic name."

What I find are two types of literacy and social practice, emergent from divergent locations of power and culture, yet entwined: on the one hand, the sailors' imperialistic sleight of hand, which, in the name of a "universal mission" to civilize others, creates and enforces difference; on the other hand, the social practices of the colonized who, despite being subject to these processes of exclusion, or perhaps because of the experience, struggle for some practical idea of cooperation and common humanity, of trying to "get along with everyone." For my grandfather, migration represented this possibility.

I believe that he carried this idea until his last days at his final destination in Queens, New York, in an apartment complex that had, 60 years earlier, received a petition to keep him and my grandmother out because they were a mixed couple. They did not leave, and they probably outlived all the signers. Eventually my grandfather also achieved some approximation of a communitarian ideal, a supportive network of friends and family that traverses class and cultural boundaries. His idea of "universalism" and his expressed beliefs that "we are all God's children" and that "we are all equally human and capable" did not originate from a desire to master, but rather out of dislocation and poverty.

As an immigrant in the U.S. Navy, my grandfather, I believe, saw the ocean as both a figure and an inspiration for the immigrant experience: between the periphery and center and between cultures. It represents those spaces that exist in proximity to, but are not completely controlled by, more settled ways of knowing and being; they are sites where both unlearning, a questioning of assumptions, and new learning may take place. It is also the realm of unstable and evolving identities. The fact of transition, of movement, afforded my grandfather the opportunity to begin reconciling conflicting notions of what it means to be both Filipino and American in order to create community where community did not exist for him.

For my grandfather the water was deeply imbued with emotional content, connoting both loss and social transformation. In the narratives of my former fifth-grade students' other spaces, such as the fields, streets, border, refugee camps, and real and imagined homelands, suggest similar dynamics and states of mind—where convention is not so pervasive and all-encompassing that it obscures the possibility to envision alternatives to one's situation.

I think of how easily, how naturally, my grandfather's migration sounds like a narrative of intergenerational upward mobility through hard work and sacrifice. I still have trouble letting go of this parable. It is challenging for me to see his life in its full complexity and contradiction, to hold in my mind the sense of historical plausibility and idiosyncratic personal odyssey that was his story and is my story to (re)discover, to realize his life could have taken very different turns and to understand both what was gained and what was lost on that trip across the Pacific.

I believe that it is also challenging to view the lives and learning of contemporary urban and immigrant students with equal complexity. Nevertheless, this may be the work that needs to be done if we are to transform these students' too often ascribed secondary status in the educational system and create alternative communitarian spaces conducive to their capacities for self-definition, resistance, and social empowerment. It may also be the work necessary for us to surpass our own boundaries and grow as educators.

Acknowledgments

THIS BOOK WOULD NOT HAVE BEEN possible were it not for my access to a number of professional communities. At the University of Pennsylvania, where I did my graduate studies, I benefited from the pioneering work of veteran teacher researchers who had committed substantial portions of their lives to educational equity. The Carnegie Foundation for the Advancement for Teaching and Learning introduced me to more inspiring teachers and also provided me with crucial time in which to write about my life in the classroom. I am humbled to have participated in the Future of Minority Studies Research Project, whose scholars modeled what it means to be "intellectual activists" and gave me confidence that it might be worthy to think about their theoretical advancements with respect to experience and identity alongside my own work with elementary students. From more of a distance, I admire members of the Filipino American National Historical Society, who tutored me in the value of my own heritage and the social significance of individual stories. Both in my former teaching contexts and in my current job at Indiana University, Bloomington, I have been blessed to have supportive colleagues.

Carol Collins at Teachers College Press and Amy Bauman provided thoughtful and concise editorial advice. My close friend Gregory Wolmart responded to initial drafts of the manuscript with challenging honesty and critical acumen. Stephanie Carter also provided perceptive feedback. Monica Muñante was a steadfast source of practical support, patience, and companionship. Vivian Gadsen set the standard for a professional life that combines the mind and heart. At the center of this work is Susan L. Lytle, a mentor with tremendous intellectual integrity and compassion. My parents always offered love and support. And finally, I am deeply indebted to the generosity of the children and families who opened their lives to me. This book is dedicated to them.

Immigrant Students and Literacy

The National Mythology and Urban Teaching

T HIS BOOK IS THE RESULT of my work as a fifth-grade teacher researcher at a neighborhood elementary school in a midsize city in California between the years 1998 and 2001. On the most general level, I address classic questions that have continued relevance and urgency for education in the United States:

- How may teachers respond to a student population characterized by unprecedented cultural and experiential diversity?
- How may public schools become a means of empowerment and self-determination for children from immigrant, migrant, and refugee backgrounds?

"UNITED IN DIVERSITY": THE RHETORIC AND REALITY

In August 1999, a group of students, teachers, and parents painted a mural across the street from our school that provides a useful visual aid for introducing some of the challenges and possibilities of such inquiries. The mural depicts five ethnic quilts, representing Chinese, African Americans, Filipino/as, Hmong, and Mexicans, respectively, all within the auspices of an unfurled American flag. A banner with the phrase "We the People United in Diversity" adorns the top of the mural and a dedication to the school community frames the bottom. The image most likely evokes a range of emotions relating to our most cherished values of democracy and pluralism. It may be considered a symbolic variation on the "cultural mosaic," stirring some of our deepest desires to imagine our country as a land of tolerance and equal opportunity—one of the foundational myths of our immigrant country's national narrative.

The mural is more than a mere reflection of a national mythology. Many families, both native and foreign born, continue to pin their hopes on public education as a means of increasing the life opportunities of future generations. It is also a vision that motivates many sincere educational-reform efforts and a guiding ideal that must be articulated and revised if those students who are most vulnerable in our school systems are to take full advantage of all that this country has to offer. As in any consensual framework, however, what is left out is as important as what is obviously celebrated. A critical reading of the mural might point out a more complicated reality. The colorful ethnic quilts are represented in a symmetrical and analogical relationship to one another, giving an impression of harmony while eliding histories of conquest, conflict, and inequality. The various ethnoracial representations are perhaps subordinate to an implicitly European American norm that remains unmarked. "Tagging"periodically surfaces, is painted over, and resurfaces in and around the borders of the mural, a reminder that some people may not buy into the mural's message.

If it seems too strong to suggest that there is an absolute disparity between the rhetoric and the reality of opportunity, only a cursory look at the statistics of our school is needed to reveal how far we have yet to go to achieve this ideal. The school is located on the city's south side, in a neighborhood that, according to the 2000 census, is the most segregated from the city's population of "non-Hispanic" whites. During the years in which I worked as a teacher researcher, the school housed roughly 1,100 students. More than 95% were eligible for free lunch. With few exceptions, many of these were from families of the working poor. Their parents and guardians often worked in several low-wage, unstable jobs in order to make a living. Many of the students, in turn, were "latchkey kids," and many played an instrumental role in fulfilling domestic responsibilities. If they were contributors at home and in the neighborhood, at school they remained objects for remediation—or "clients," as they were described by educational companies—for the latest curricular programs. The students consistently scored, on average, significantly below their middle-class peers on standardized tests. Less than 25% of the students in the entering ninth-grade class of the local high school continued on for a college degree. In these and other ways the conditions of our school and neighborhood resembled the conditions of many urban schools and neighborhoods.

Another line of interpretation, drawn from more recent developments in cultural studies, may take note of how the "groups" on the mural are represented as bounded and internally uniform—as fixed and static as the concrete onto which they are emblazoned. Our social identities, we are coming to learn, may always be in the act of becoming, more fluid and composed through the ever-evolving affiliations of our lives. Even those ethnoracial designations that seem to have a historical persistence are reformulated and elaborated on to address more expansive and flexible notions of human agency. The apparently fixed categories on the mural downplay these productive energies and with them the possibilities for intercultural cooperation and transformation, especially in a school where the students speak more than 14 home languages, claim multifaceted identities, share a vibrant youth culture, and inherit rich literary and activist traditions.

My concern, of course, is not with the mural per se, but with how the image it conveys has become reified in schools. Educational reforms typically do not take into account those histories of inequality that constrain students. They also do not build on the rich experiences and legacies (Gadsden, 1992) students bring to school. Yet these are the very social and empirical realities that those of us who work in urban schools must negotiate. What is thus symbolically absent from the mural reflects a primary paradox of teaching. We encounter daily a system that reinforces an idea of deprivation: of community decay, teacher incompetence, parental neglect, and ultimately student failure. At the same time, daily, we encounter children, young adults, and families who are responding to their circumstances, including this pervasive discourse of deprivation, with creativity and promise. Teachers may hold in their minds at once received understandings of student deficit and perceived understandings of student capacity and potential.

CLASSROOM PRACTICE AND CULTURAL CONTEXT

One arguably dominant response to this paradox is to compartmentalize diversity, as we can see represented pictorially on the mural with the ethnic groups bounded and internally uniform. We tend to agree that our differences should be tolerated—even affirmed—but can the students read, have they acquired basic skills, and are their test scores rising? The dominant view is that the knowledge needed to bring students up to par must be proved, imported to schools, and codified as professional development, especially in districts serving low-income and minority populations. Prospective teachers should be "trained" in "scientifically proved best practices." Veteran teachers should also be well versed in the latest research-based methods and programs. Attention to issues of culture may be necessary for the psychosocial well-being of students, but the methodological bias is that effective knowledge for teaching and learning can be abstracted from the actual social-cultural contexts of teaching and learning.

Although this top-down paradigm may have brought necessary attention to underresourced schools, schools that might otherwise have been ignored, often it ironically renders pedagogically irrelevant both the complexities and the promise of multiculturalism and literacy. For example, the current aggrandizement of teaching methods and programs catered toward high-stakes tests has the effect of homogenizing classroom practice and devaluing the resources and experiences students bring to school. Test scores *may* rise, but such an approach may also inadvertently limit students' full potential and stymie educators' ability to learn from the rich diversity of their classrooms. Gains in tests scores are not enough. I believe it is useful to make the distinction between teaching with the goal of having students register progress on discrete measures and teaching with the desire to speak to students' cultural identities, honor the realities of their lives and prepare them for college. The former may be addressed prescriptively; the latter requires vision and a more sophisticated understanding of what constitutes educational knowledge.

In contrast to transmission models of teaching, I document an organic approach to educational knowledge and practice. I argue that sound knowledge about the lives and learning of students may be generated from the day-to-day collaborative work of teachers and students as they adopt an inquiry stance into those very experiences that have been repressed, obscured, or excluded. In this book I suggest that this curricular work is part of an alternative "second classroom" that runs in tandem with and sometimes counter to the mandated curriculum. Marilyn Cochran-Smith and Susan L. Lytle (2001) characterize these "processes of knowledge construction" as a matter of "building, interrogating, elaborating, and critiquing conceptual frameworks that link action and problem-posing to the immediate context as well as to larger social, cultural, and political issues" (pp. 51–52). In this more horizontal model, the classroom is conceptualized as a space of shared inquiry and the diversity of the student population as an epistemic advantage, rather than a hindrance, to formulating alternative theories of practice that will facilitate the success of students. Issues of culture and power are not a cordoned-off area of analysis. Rather they are integrated into the educational development of students and the professional development of teachers, informing our school-based literacy practices, how we imagine a broader understanding of curricula, and ultimately what we consider the purposes of education in a democratic society.

I suggest that sober and cogent accounts of the conditions of teaching and learning in urban schools is necessary to awaken greater self-understanding of educators and an affirmative consciousness about what may be required to enable all students to flourish. Teacher research, or more precisely, the process of becoming and living the life of a teacher researcher, is a promising avenue for such a venture. This book is thus a situated analysis in at least two senses of the term. The analysis challenges schools to live up to the ideals they purport rhetorically, especially the progressive American ideals of equal access and opportunity. Yet it also originates in a location embedded in the very realities it wishes to consider, not some seemingly transcendent, disinterested point free of the consequences of one's evaluations and actions. I strive to reconcile university-based research with full immersion in the life-stream of an urban classroom and neighborhood, including both its fluidity and constraints.

THIS BOOK AND ITS ORGANIZATION

As a full-time classroom teacher, I have taught every subject and lived a spectrum of experiences and emotions related to my job. For example, perhaps my most salient memories of teaching are about the daily irreverence, laughter, and joy of working with the children and their families. This book touches on this aspect of the job. Following teacher researchers Marsha Pincus (2005) and Bob Fecho (2003), I also engage the "dissonances," struggles, and dilemmas of teaching because they bring into relief issues of power that are generative points from which to arrive at new understandings and take new actions. I do not strive to provide complete phenomenological rendition of my teaching. I offer instead an interpretive slice of the overall picture. My specific focus is the role that immigrant stories may play in the classroom.

However, in this book I also do not aim to "instruct" in any conventional sense. Instead of putting forward either a prescriptive or comprehensive pedagogical doctrine, I provide an account of a practitioner methodology that foregrounds the experiential and cultural resources of teachers and students. I thus invite teachers to imagine their own classrooms as collaborative sites of inquiry that may inform their practice *and* have general relevance to the larger educational community. It is in this challenge for teachers to adopt a more expansive role for themselves as not merely appliers, but also purveyors and generators of both empirical and conceptual knowledge, that I hope this book finds resonance.

The chapters of the book are organized into three parts to unfold as a widening of vision and opening up to and engagement with the world. It begins with an inward-looking perspective, with an exploration of my own identity and the awakening of my drive to become a teacher researcher (Part I). I then turn outward, to focus, first, on individual children in a community of learners and, second, on the teacher's role in that community, viewing the community as composed of simply learners then as made up of individuals whose lives are intertwined (Part II). I close with a description of how I have modified my own professional self-understanding in light of what I have learned from my students and some considerations for future generations of teacher researchers (Part III).

This book suggests that it is by adopting a critical-inquiry stance into one's practice that a generative dialectic is created between what is and what might be, because what *is* is often woefully inadequate; and the urgency to create new meanings and practices on a day-to-day, face-to-face basis cannot await outside policy prescriptions and research "implications."

Perhaps more than anything else, the book may be a meditation on the significance of relationships: the relationships between students and teachers, students to one another, and students to literacy and the world. As the limitations of "scientifically based" teaching practices and one-size-fits-all curriculum are becoming exposed, there has been renewed interest in the importance of learning communities in diverse contexts. With its ultimate call for urban teacher researchers to begin thinking of themselves as having an emergent professional/political identity and as being part of a vibrant intellectual culture, I hope this book contributes to a relational (re)turn in educational research, policy, and practice.

PART I

The Power of Inquiry

P ART I DESCRIBES HOW I DEVELOPED my inquiry stance. I suggest that my professional growth entailed learning to trust that my experiences with my students in the classroom could become a valuable intellectual resource. Chapter 1 situates my work in traditions of teacher research. I argue that both teachers and students generate "knowledge of practice" (Cochran-Smith & Lytle, 1999), deriving conceptual understandings based on their own experiences living and learning in urban neighborhoods and schools. In the lexicon of teacher researchers, Chapter 1 is *a story of the question*, relating the key memories in my own professional journey as an urban educator that would eventually lead me to ask, What happens when I invite children from immigrant and refugee families to generate literacy practices from their own experiences? In the rest of the book I describe how students can bring their rich cultural and experiential traditions to school and use them to develop literacies.

Chapter 2 introduces Celso, one of my students during my first year as a fifth-grade teacher researcher, and explores the role that storytelling, memory, and the sharing of familial history play as components of both a method of inquiry and a means of creating a sense of community within the class.

In Chapter 3 I discuss my interactions with one child, Carmen, to illustrate the sense of failure and lost opportunity from which the remainder of my work grew. I conclude the chapter by describing how my experiences with Carmen helped me conceptualize my teaching as the interplay between two classrooms: a "first classroom" during regular school hours and an alternative "second classroom" during the margins and in-between periods of the day that builds curricula around the students' identities.

CHAPTER 1

"From the Heart to the World and Back Again"

Negotiating the Boundaries

> Why didn't you reach out, touch us with your fingers, delay the sound bite, the lesson, until you knew who we were. . . . No song, no literature, no poem full of vitamins, no history connected to experience that you can pass along to help us start strong?
>   —Toni Morrison, Nobel Lecture in Literature, 1993

O VER THE COURSE OF MY TEACHING career, my investigation into my students' experiences and my own reflections about the relationship between teaching and research became inextricably linked contexts of inquiry. The negotiations that children from immigrant, migrant, and refugee families undertake as they adapt to schools have helped me clarify the pressures that urban teacher researchers may feel as they negotiate the worlds of academia, research, policy, and their respective school sites. While I do not intend to draw too tight an analogy, I do suggest that how we respond to diversity is both informed by and informs what we value as knowledge in the classroom. This book is one attempt to unsettle and make more porous commonplace distinctions between academic theory and the everyday theorizing of urban life, between the intellectual work of teaching and the labor of research, and between the realities of immigrant children and the experiences of those who are invested in their futures. Teacher research provides a unique avenue for learning from diverse students, who help us come to a deeper appreciation of our own cultural work and its potential contributions to the field of education.

FROM THE LOCATION OF THE CLASSROOM

In 1991, fresh out of my undergraduate education, I went to Houston, Texas, to teach first grade. I had very little preparation. I began a month into the year; the class that had been created for me was labeled a "transitional" first-grade class in a "low-performing" Title I school. The school had an advanced track, which was composed of designated gifted students who did not attend a nearby magnet program. Then there were regular classes. All the teachers from the regular classes selected the "lowest" or "most challenging" students from their own rosters to put in the transitional class with the least experienced member of the faculty. My first group of six- and seven-year-old children had been sifted through at least four levels of tracking and they were from a highly segregated and underresourced neighborhood.

This time I spent as a first-grade teacher laid the foundation for my career in education. My memories evoke a predictable range of emotions, as I recall moments of frustration as well as the incomparable rewards of witnessing emerging readers and writers. Some of my strongest convictions about education have their roots in what I learned from my Houston colleagues, many of whom were veteran urban teachers and administrators who combined academic rigor with unconditional nurturance and support. However, I have one memory that for me speaks above all to the importance of seeing my teaching as connected to the social and political contexts of schooling. It is of the responses of some children to high-stakes mandated testing.

During the first half of the school year, the students were required to take a fairly extensive state examination that involved, among other tasks, reading long paragraphs and marking answers by filling in circles on a test sheet. Many of the children were from immigrant families and spoke English as a second language. Because kindergarten was not required, several students had just a few months of formal schooling and were beginning to learn the alphabet and how to write their names. I had been scrambling to give many of the children additional attention through the school's referral process. All the students were selected to be in my class so they would not take instructional time away from the "more advanced" students.

The children would invariably react harshly to the tests, despite my efforts to offer reassurance, to at once encourage them to do their best while at the same time communicating to them that the tests did not reflect their potential or my belief in them. Some would cry; some would fall ill with nausea; others would display uncharacteristic anger, panic, and confrontational behavior. I felt as if their academic identities were already being forged in a crucible of failure and remediation, at the age of 6. Their reactions would, in turn, provoke my own anxiety. As a teacher and therefore an extension of the school, I felt myself complicit with a system that induced social suffering.

At the time I had an emerging, if inchoate, awareness that the struggle of many of the children had very little to do with their abilities or desires to succeed. This awareness was all but crowded out by the unremitting stresses that accompany teaching in an underresourced school. Despite my efforts and the then-popular euphemistic slogan "All children can learn," I knew that the tracks were, to a large extent, intractable. Several of my colleagues would attempt to comfort me by suggesting that if I could only make a difference in one child's life, I should be satisfied. "What else could be done when the parents themselves were neither educated nor cared about their own children's education?" was not an uncommon misconception. "Just make sure to thoroughly document the students' failures" was a piece of advice I received repeatedly. Urban teaching was ironically thought of as a "selfless" profession in which nurturing individuals could become low-level technicians who executed curricula to "needy" children. If this was done well, they could absolve themselves of all further responsibilities. They had met their professional duty.

Without the perspective to gain a deeper understanding of issues such as social reproduction, and perhaps more important cultural production (Levinson, Foley, & Holland, 1996) and educational activism (Quartz, Olsen, & Duncan-Andrade, 2004), I struggled vainly to find the perfect "practice" to ameliorate my students' educational circumstances, going so far as to send myself across country to attend a 10-day seminar on a remedial, scripted reading program. I needed vision, a way to comprehend the complexities of my environment. Instead, I was offered narrow approaches to teaching that only exacerbated my sense of fragmentation, isolation, and failure.

FROM THE LOCATION OF THE UNIVERSITY

During my first year at the University of Pennsylvania, my professors invited me to reflect back upon my experiences in Houston. I began to understand how my beginning years of teaching were colored by a deficit ideology that generated distorted understandings of students, teaching, and learning. The feelings of inadequacy, both the incompetency that the children must have felt and my own sense that I was failing them, were at least in part the result of unquestioned assumptions and a lack of contextual nuance about what constitutes an empowering learning environment. The tests did not encompass the children's particular life stories: their linguistic and class backgrounds and their unfamiliarity with formal schooling or school-like practices. They coerced the students into trying to conform to a narrow standard, one that denied their personal histories; it was a denial, I believe, that disadvantaged the children from the beginning and that compromised their academic potentials.

Instead of framing the children's struggle as the result of individual or family and, by implication, cultural deficit, I became poignantly aware of how larger structures of social stratification became inscribed onto their very bodies. The processes of school categorization were a form of "symbolic violence" (Bourdieu, 1993) that caused immediate physiological effects and tensions, which would potentially have long-term consequences in the children's lives. The students' initial encounters with school were being penetrated by power dynamics that, by proxy, I felt but lacked both the immediate personal familiarity with and the conceptual vocabulary to name. If the children were to have access to a higher education, they would most likely have to engage in a process of "unlearning" what schools were continually communicating to them: that they were failures. My critical consciousness of these issues involved transforming previous feelings of inadequacy into a desire for advocacy. I then gained a new appreciation for the ways in which teachers I had admired, many of whom shared the backgrounds of their students, mitigated the social suffering of children through subtle, rarely recognized interactions and also through assertive acts of resistance. Their astute awareness of the needs and capabilities of the children was a deeper knowledge born out of a sustained commitment to the school and neighborhood.

One of our first challenges as teacher researchers is to inquire into and often call into question our own taken-for-granted assumptions about teaching and learning. This is why we often begin with an exploration of our own educational and literacy histories. Far from self-indulgence, this ongoing process of reflection and reflexivity has direct bearing on the conceptual frameworks we employ to learn from and with our students. It was therefore important that my transformation in graduate school was personal as well as professional. My inquiries into teaching and my investigation of my own ethnicity were inseparable. Growing up, I lacked the institutional support to explore the Filipino side of my identity. To be "academic" and to be "ethnic" seemed mutually exclusive endeavors.

FROM THE LOCATION OF MY PAST

It was not until I took a course on multicultural education, in which I read Sonia Nieto's landmark work *Affirming Diversity* (1996), that I began to appreciate the epistemic significance of my own cultural identity. Inspired by the case studies in Nieto's book, I interviewed my grandfather to understand his own immigrant narrative in light of theories of ethnicity and literacy. I would later develop this work in a seminar with the folklorist Margaret Mills. Although I was not aware of it at the time, it was also my first foray into using the ethnic/immigrant narrative as a research method. I began to reconstruct my personal and familial narrative and juxtapose it with my own experiences of teaching children.

The assignments were more than a sentimental exercise in nostalgia or an ersatz discovery of my roots. The epistemic role of my investigation involved revealing aspects of my family history that had been buried beneath layers of assimilation. It was a case of the grandchild trying to remember what had been forgotten, repressed, or willfully distanced by previous generations. I attempted to translate into a more coherent narrative my grandfather's stories, his silences, and my own visceral emotions about him. In the process, I unearthed and questioned deeply inculcated beliefs about what it means to be "literate" and "educated." I discovered the gaps, contradictions, and tensions within my own family's story of "intergenerational upward mobility." I also became sensitized to how individuals and frequently whole populations become branded as "illiterate" or "subliterate" because of the assumptions beneath what Brian Street (1984) has labeled the autonomous model of literacy. Instead of seeing my grandfather as merely a person who was limited by his upbringing, I understood the ways in which he strategically culled what he needed from multiple linguistic and cultural resources in order to adapt to precarious social circumstances and become an agent in his own postcolonial migration.

In this instance, academic theories on the varied and ideological nature of literacy (Street, 1993) merged with my own personal, if undeveloped, intuitions to arrive at a more complete understanding of both what was lost and what was gained in my own family's immigrant history. This understanding, in turn, would eventually inform the way I conceptualized a pedagogy that strove to enable contemporary students from immigrant, migrant, and refugee families become more effective agents in their own educational development by drawing upon their own life experiences, values, and literate practices. What would it mean to think about classroom literacy as varied sets of "social practices" that "are themselves rooted in conceptions of knowledge, identity, and being" (Street, 2001, p. 7)?

BACK TO THE URBAN CLASSROOM

In graduate school I learned about the potential of education to lead to personal transformation. But as I became further immersed in my studies, I felt myself being pulled back to urban neighborhoods and schools. Even though the university is situated in an urban environment, the differences between the elite campus and its immediate working-class environs were, predictably, stark. The differences were, in my mind, a physical manifestation of the differences in power and prestige between the world of "research and theory" and the world of "practice." My desire to write my dissertation from the location of the classroom was more than a social responsibility or an opportunity to "put theory into practice." Rather, it was based on an emerging conviction that the experiences of urban teachers and students might also inform the way I theorized the practice of educational scholarship. I saw myself as benefiting from the rich tradition of practitioner inquiry initiated by my mentors at Penn, including Elizabeth Canafio, Vanessa Brown, Marsha Pincus, Bob Fecho, and Diana Waff. They were all inspiring teacher researchers and writers who were committed to urban communities. The more abstract realms of interpretation, critical reflection, deliberation, and intervention are not divorced from practice, I came to understand, but in fact nourished by the life-world of the classroom and neighborhood.

I finally decided to integrate the personal and professional by taking a position in a historic Filipino American community in California. During my first evening in a motel, I met Guadalupe* while she helped her

---

* To protect the identity of the children described throughout this book, I have used pseudonyms rather than their real names and changed some minor biographical details.

mother clean the rooms. The following day, when I visited what was to be my school site, I ran into Guadalupe once again, on the playground. I was struck by the realization that there were very different cultural and class-based understandings of childhood. For Guadalupe, part of being a child involved laboring to help reduce her mother's workload and stress. I would subsequently think about this coincidence—the coincidence of seeing a child in two environments that were separate in my mind because of the limitations of my own class background—whenever I would hear teachers ascribe to children attributes such as *lazy*. It is a reminder of just how ingrained is our conception of a separation between intellectual work and physical and emotional labor, even though, I have come to believe, schools often prepare children like Guadalupe to perform the very work for which they are penalized.

Guadalupe's pedagogical challenge to me was to discover the knowledge born of the encounter between worlds. Would it be possible to imagine her life experiences not as a deficit, but as a resource and a potential theoretical orientation to the world, one that could deepen my own understanding of teaching and learning in an ethnically diverse neighborhood? Many of our students have been uprooted and come to us in the process of their adjusting to a new environment. Their families have migrated both across and within national borders and cultural boundaries in search of security. The children often participate in informal systems of family and neighborhood reciprocity in order to help their families survive. They feel a sense of responsibility not only to their immediate family, but also to networks of kin that extend beyond the immediate neighborhood to various diaspora communities around the world.

These types of experiences or "embodied knowledge" were the "raw material" to fashion identities (Mohanty, 1997, p. 205). They could develop into what the Chicana literary critic Paula Moya identifies as experientially mediated knowledge, or, quoting Cherri L. Moraga, as a "theory of flesh" born out of the "physical realities of our [women of color] lives," such as "skin color" and "the land and concrete we grew up on" (Moya, 2000, pp. 91–92). For the children in our school neighborhood, these realities might include their migrations; their work in motels, fields, and flea markets; their encounters with racism, severely overcrowded and under-resourced schools, low expectations, and poverty; and their everyday lives on the streets of a segregated California barrio.

When children come to class, however, they are often led to believe that these realities don't matter, except as a barrier to learning. Many are reticent at the beginning, eager to defer to the wisdom of teachers and administrators. With persistent disappointment, this reticence may evolve into feelings of frustration, disengagement, and eventually disenchantment.

What would it mean to develop curricula that acknowledge our students' unique social identities, not as problems, but rather as profound sources of knowledge that could help us illuminate aspects of our shared world and inform the ways in which we conceptualize our pedagogies? How might the students' own "subjective experience" help educators "criticize and rewrite dominant and oppressive narratives" (Alcoff & Mohanty, 2006, pp. 4–5). What would it mean to learn from the "epistemic privilege" of the students' perspectives, described as "a special advantage with respect to possessing or acquiring knowledge about how fundamental aspects of our society operate to sustain matrices of power" (Moya, 2001, p. 479)? One of the biggest challenges of urban teachers is to help create an environment in which all children and young adults feel empowered to critically reflect and draw upon the realities of their lives. What it takes to create such an environment is not simply a matter of setting the conditions for knowledge to occur, but is a type of knowledge *in and of itself*. It involves, among other things, cultivating the affective and intellectual bonds that enable students to recognize that they too possess valuable knowledge to bring to bear upon their educational development. Without trust, this type of cultural and relational work is impossible.

A PROFESSIONAL COMMUNITY

This work also requires a professional development infrastructure. While I worked to create a community in my classroom, I was simultaneously on a parallel, related quest to find a professional community, "a home," that would engage questions that I found germane to teaching and learning in urban schools. There were many colleagues in my school site from whom I learned a tremendous amount, among them an administrator who valued conflict management over punishment, a teacher who proved that our students could win a highly competitive academic pentathlon, a local professor who visited regularly to remind students that college was for them, and a number of teachers from the neighborhood who once again demonstrated that an affirmation of diversity and academic rigor were twin ideals. Nevertheless, there were no official mechanisms to enable teachers to share their knowledge and inquiries. The dominant professional development model was one of transmission, in which outside experts trained us in the latest research.

I eventually had to create what I was looking for. My professional community, however, spanned social, institutional, and disciplinary boundaries. It included teachers, professors from various departments, activists, community members, and students—a collection of disparately located kindred spirits who informed my thinking. The community was a function of shared interest rather than professional affiliation or disciplinary allegiance. Too often, however, it was also an exertion of will, an internal conversation that did not necessarily reflect my day-to-day existence, which remained professionally isolated. I found myself betwixt and between the world of academia and urban schools, in search of a mutually informing and complementary axis of interpretation. I wanted my classroom experiences to be more than an object of reflection for myself or for others, to actually infuse and condition my research methodology and theory of practice.

THE POWER OF STORIES

This book is written as a series of critical stories and representative anecdotes through which I attempt to explore what it means to teach and learn in a diverse urban neighborhood. Why did I choose this approach? Some university-based researchers may disregard the stories of teachers because they are not rigorous, are too subjective, cannot be generalized, are self-absorbed, and so on. Why even engage in the "risky" (Lytle, 1993) and involved work of a teacher researcher if it does not seemingly produce immediate outcomes? Why tell stories from and about the classroom?

These critiques warrant a response and a few remarks about my own use of narrative and emphasis on the imagination and speculative thought *as* educational scholarship. By *imagination*, I do not mean something fanciful and out of touch with reality. I have more in mind what Maxine Greene (1994) discusses when she writes of imagination as "a reaching out towards alternative ways of being human, of being in the world" (p. 24). It is the imagination required to speculate about and enact alternative pedagogical practices that are more conducive to the flourishing of those students who are the most vulnerable in our school system.

As many anthropologists and folklorists might point out, we already enter our classrooms with storylike expectations that influence self-understanding and affect practice. Both in my own life and in the lives of my students, there is the archetypal American story of upward mobility for immigrant families through hard work and sacrifice. But as I suggested in my narrative about Guadalupe, many of my students work hard in order to help their families survive. Many also work in school and have surpassed academic standards. Yet these sacrifices do not necessarily translate into empowerment in our school systems. How do we begin to make sense of this contradiction?

The most common way is to reassert the dominant narrative. If children are not successful, it must be because they still have not worked hard enough or made enough sacrifices—the meritocracy thesis—or because they essentially lack the ability because of a personal or family deficit. When children attempt to square their own experiences with this pervasive narrative of how their school lives should unfold, they may begin to accept themselves as failures in school. How do we then begin to imagine alternatives?

One possibility is to recognize the students' experiences as a source of knowledge and a point from which to theorize practice. It was striking to me that many of the students' narratives had an almost epic quality, being at once deeply personal and tied to group histories of both oppression and empowerment. They were about survival, unimaginable loss, separation from home and community, and continued social exclusion and estrangement. They were also about possibility, social action, and hope. I felt that the only real way to honor the power, immediacy, and truth of their stories was through retelling them. When I was able to leave myself open to the experiences of the students by developing a pedagogy of listening (Schultz, 2003), allowing them to inscribe their own individual stories into the collective text of the class, they began to shape my own stance as an educator. The narratives were a form of memory, but they were also a form of countermemory, set against bureaucratic means of recording the students' educational experiences. I believe they helped provide a richer context for teaching and learning, one that better enabled children to "start strong," as Toni Morrison put it.

Students (and teachers) write not only *from* experience but also *for* experience; storytelling becomes an ongoing process of inquiry and discovery that is potentially generative. Maria, a student described in this book, once characterized her writing process by stating that her words went "from the heart to the world and back again." This phrase eloquently captures the dialectical and intersubjective process of coming into consciousness through collaborative inquiry. The students produce literacy practices from their "hearts," from that which is experienced most immediately and viscerally. These experiences may only be partially understood, existing at a repressed or intuitive level. But in the process of making meaning—through speaking, through putting words on paper, through dance, drama, and the recitation of verse—the children come in contact with a larger world. This world might include the experiences of other members of the classroom community and the wisdom of their ancestors and kin who provide a sense of lived history, of characters in novels whose fictional lives resonate with their own, of what teachers may have to offer when they expose their full humanity beyond their institutional roles, and of everything we may put under an expansive understanding of curriculum. When this curriculum is responsive to who the children are, to the physical realities of their lives, their words return with new import, enabling them to arrive at new understandings of their relationships to their social worlds and awakening a fuller sense of imaginative and then actual possibility. This, in turn, enables them to have qualitatively different experiences of their worlds, engendering new forms of school literacy practice and new identities and opening new vistas for investigation and self-discovery.

CHAPTER 2

Celso's Secret Box

Creating Community Through Shared Stories

Break a vase, and the love that reassembles the fragments is stronger than that love which took its symmetry for granted when it was whole . . . and if the pieces are disparate, ill-fitting, they contain more pain than their original sculpture.

—Derek Walcott, *What the Twilight Says*

STORIES OF DEATH AND LOSS are not uncommon in urban classrooms. Too often they elicit merely stock responses and expressions of sympathy. As a teacher I learned that it required deliberate mindfulness to step back from daily pressures to listen and try to respond adequately to what individual children were going through. While I was in the process of trying to get to know 35 new fifth-grade students on the first day of school, one child, Celso, told me that his father had passed away over the summer. Later that day, he sought more of my attention. Walking up to a map of the Philippine Islands, he pointed to the southern island of Mindanao.

"That's where my father was from."

"How old was he?" I asked.

"Ninety-one," he replied.

I shared with Celso that my grandfather was from Mindanao as well. He smiled. It was the beginning of our connection. I would eventually see pictures from his father's funeral: Celso, 10 years old, uncomfortably fitted in a jacket and tie, standing by the open casket, accepting condolences. He was with friends and family, including his mother, brother, and two sisters.

Around the same time as the funeral, during the summer of 1998, I had been preparing to move to a midsize city in California. I had chosen to move there because of its ethnically diverse populations of immigrant,

migrant, and refugee students. I wanted to teach and conduct research in an area steeped in Filipino/a American history. I recall trying to explain my decision to my family. My grandparents seemed at once supportive and at the same time a little skeptical of my desires. They wondered what was to be gained in California. After my grandfather had migrated to California from the Philippines in the 1920s, he decided to leave that state, partly because of its antimiscegenation laws. He arrived in New York City, the trip resulting from the fortuitous stop of a navy ship. He lived in New York for more than sixty years with his wife, my grandmother. Together, they raised seven children. Now here I was moving to California to return intellectually and imaginatively to some nebulous and remote site of collective history. I was leaving my grandfather, 3,000 miles behind and in faltering health, in order to discover him again.

THE MANONGS AND MANANGS

Celso's father had been about the same age as my grandfather. They emigrated from the same region of the Philippines during the same time period for roughly the same reason: poverty. Maybe they knew each other. Actually, this is not as unlikely as it seems, since there were so few Filipino immigrants in the United States at that time. For those interested in Filipino/a American history, Celso's father and my grandfather were known as *pioneers, old-timers,* or *manongs.* In the Ilocano language, *manong* means "old brother" and *manang* "older sister." These are designations of respect for elders. They have also come to label a generation, a wave of newcomers to the United States who performed stoop labor in the fields and worked in Alaskan canneries and fishing boats, the restaurant industry, and many other low-wage service sectors. They were a tractable labor force and had an ambiguous social status. They were originally designated *nationals,* neither *aliens* nor *citizens.* The signifier *Filipino* has never denoted a stable, coherent referent in official racial taxonomies. To this day, Filipino/as often defy institutional categories.

Between roughly 1920 and 1950, the *manongs* and *manangs* were stereotyped as unlettered barrio folk. Along with the straitjacket of being labeled as illiterate, a host of linguistic trappings were associated with them that, when taken together, created a Filipino/a identity that fueled exploitation and rationalized nativist violence. When Filipinos were perceived as taking jobs and dating White women, there were anti-Filipino riots in a number of California towns. Many *manongs,* like Celso's father, would start families later in life because of antimiscegenation laws and a pronounced gender imbalance, the ratio of Filipinos to Filipinas being roughly 10 to 1.

However, the *manongs* and *manangs* were not merely recipients of historical processes. They also made history, as colonial subjects who, out of economic necessity, moved from the periphery to the center, forging sustainable lives for themselves while defining new ways of being Filipina/o and of being American (Bohulano Mabalon, 2005). In the more celebrated narratives, they paved the way for future generations by sowing the seeds of community and initiating the struggle for Filipina/o American civil rights.

DIFFERENT PATHS, DIFFERENT STORIES

Despite parallels, my grandfather and Celso's father made very different decisions, emblematic of the diversity within any immigrant group. These decisions had profound effects on the experiences of future generations. I grew up on the East Coast, not knowing there was such a thing as a Filipino/a American culture or experience. It was not until graduate school that I began to consciously foreground the Filipino side of my identity, trying to unearth aspects of my family's history that had been buried beneath layers of assimilation. I became what Leny Mendoza Strobel (2000) calls a "Born Again Filipino."

I decided to interview my grandfather. Many of his stories were subtle and ironic. For example, in one of my last conversations with him, he told me of his youthful desires to become an actor. After being turned down repeatedly, he was finally offered a role at a local Brooklyn playhouse. It was, stereotypically, that of a "houseboy." He did not accept the role, but a week later, in order to feed his family, he took a position as an actual houseboy for a doctor in New York City's Upper East Side. I interpret his refusal of the role as an act of resistance. It struck me that my grandfather's stage life—his imaginative self—made greater claims on his identity than did his actual job. He always thought of himself as a performance artist first. I can work as a houseboy if I have to, he seemed to say, but I am not one. My grandfather's identity was not limited by his socially ascribed role.

CELSO'S STORY

Celso's father also traveled in search of opportunities but eventually settled in California's Central Valley to raise a family. The city in which Celso lives is a cultural palimpsest. There is a Chinese population with neighborhood roots that go back to the nineteenth century. A picture from 1930 depicts the door of a downtown hotel with a sign: "Positively No Filipinos Allowed." Both Filipino/as and Mexicans organized to protest labor exploitation. Just a little more than a decade ago, a city school achieved national notoriety with a racially motivated schoolyard slaughter of mostly immigrant children. Today a steady influx of immigrants and refugees continue to work in low-wage positions, with the hope that their children and grandchildren will have greater life opportunities.

For Celso, his ethnicity was not a discovery, but a reality of which he has always been making sense. Although he circulated within a tight-knit sphere of kin, he also came in contact with people from a wide range of backgrounds, at school, in church, in the park, and at the flea market. His peers were Mexican, Filipino/a, Mexipino, Hmong, African American, Lao, Thai, and Native American. On the playground, Celso moved with facility between English and his family language, Visayan; rhymed with friends; recited his own poetry; and has been known to quote Langston Hughes, Shakespeare, and the Rock—in short, his literacy practices were diversely shaped. While Celso did not have the financial resources to partake in many aspects of consumer life, marketed to young people, he inventively drew on a range of resources to shape his own forms of youth cultural expression. For example, he began teaching himself musical instruments and with peers formed a spoken-word trio that incorporated saxophone and congas.

In the classroom, Celso produced some of his most powerful writing when he had the opportunity to articulate his own life experiences. In one example, as part of an inquiry into home and community, I invited the students to bring artifacts that represented their families. They shared their artifacts orally and then wrote essays describing the artifacts' significance. In response to this assignment, Celso composed the following in honor of his father, titled "My Dad's Secret Box":

> When my dad was still alive I didn't remember about a box. But when he passed away, my whole family scavenged into my dad's stuff. While I was looking, I found a black box inside a case. I opened the box and read everything. It was magical because it was all about his life! There were pictures of his family, pictures of him going around the world, and some envelopes and mail. It was like going on an adventure! I couldn't believe what I saw there: books, glasses, pictures, necklaces, Swiss army knives, and more!
>
> When my father was alive he was a very gracious person. He was a helpful and wonderful man. He picked asparagus in the fields for his family. He did all he could do to make his children strong, smart, gracious, and well-mannered boys and girls. Most of all he wanted us to be on our best behavior when we were at somebody's house, at church, at a party, at school and everywhere in the world!

When my dad was still alive, me, my mom, and my dad went to the Philippines. It took three days to get there! We had to go on three planes, but it was worth it! They had eggs, chicken, meat balls, and drinks. Wow! You could choose any kind of fruit juice you wanted. Finally, we got to Mindanao.

Mindanao is very poor, but full of fun and love. My dad had to go to the doctor because he could hardly breathe. Finally, he got out of the hospital. We went to our relatives. I have one sister and one aunt. My aunt works in three stores: in front of the house, in back of the house, and at the mall.

There are only two weathers in the Philippines: rainy days and sunny days. On sunny days my nose bleeds, but sometimes it doesn't. At the end of the trip, my whole family said "good bye." And then we went back to California and went to our dwelling and there we stayed.

Now that my dad has died, I will always remember him because of the black box I found. If I look through that box, I will always remember my dad.

I speculate that Celso's "scavenging" through his father's box and then discussing and writing about its contents helped him grieve. It was also an act of memory and, as such, cultural recovery. Celso begins his story by reflecting on an assortment of his father's posessions that have obvious emotional and symbolic import—letters, photos, and books. The artifacts serve as touchstones for recollection and imaginative travel. His thoughts become oriented toward the Philippines through evocative descriptions of the country's heat, his aunt's home, his father's physical well-being, and Mindanao's poverty. He eventually returns to his home in California.

CREATING COMMUNITY THROUGH NARRATIVE

As Celso and I discussed his story, it became apparent that the "secrets" of his father's box were not simply its hidden contents. They were also revealed in the interpretive work of those who examined the contents and pieced together fragments of a buried history. We learned about individual lives and group experiences that were omitted from the history textbook and the state standards. The anecdote of the secret box became one locus or embodiment of memory. Hearing and discussing the story of the secret box linked Celso to his father, my grandfather to Celso, his father to me, me to Celso, and possibly even Celso's father to my grandfather. These sets of relationships delineated the contours of a community that were like the four corners of the lid of a box, one that opened up memory and provided access to a world beyond the rote day-to-day pressures of teaching a prescribed, standardized curriculum. Through narrative Celso and I began to form a network that transverses generations and spans geographical locations, becoming a community, if initially only of two, forged by collective memory and the conveyance of shared and overlapping experience.

One of the pedagogical advantages of creating communities that cross space and time is that they nourish a rich imaginative landscape. While it is certainly true that the Philippines fertilized Celso's imagination, so did many other places, such as Alaska and Hawaii, where he has relatives. In his essays and poetry, he has even expressed a sense of affinity for places to which he has no obvious connection, such as Africa and New York. Celso described looking through his father's box as an "adventure" and "magical," keeping the Manong spirit alive. What he emphasized, more than any one place, is movement, the process of encountering people and immersing himself in new environments. His fantastical explorations were similar to his father's migrant life; they were of transit.

Still, for many migrants and refugees, every space is a potential site of conflict. I'm not sure if Celso's father went into detail with Celso about the former's more challenging experiences, such as the vehement racism marshaled against Filipino/as in the first half of the twentieth century. Perhaps he felt that Celso was too young. Maybe there was just an implicit understanding between them. But Celso did tell me that his father encouraged him to "respect and get along with everyone, no matter where they're from."

"IT'S WHAT WE HAVE SURVIVED"

I was not surprised that part of Celso's father's oral legacy was a type of universalism that might help his children negotiate foreign environments, incorporate new experiences, and build nurturing affiliations across apparent boundaries. It may also have been pragmatic simply not to discuss the more difficult truths of his life. In my work with Celso and other students from immigrant, migrant, and refugee backgrounds, I began to limn the outlines of what the anthropologist James Clifford (1997) calls a "diaspora consciousness" (p. 256), which entails a flexible notion of self and more capacious understanding of community. Community was created—both in and outside the classroom—largely through the sharing and braiding of stories. Some of my most profound moments as a fifth-grade teacher occurred when we, as a class, collaboratively inquired into familial and, by implication, cultural history. We changed school literacy from within, and it became deeply inflected with personal meaning. We planted seeds of memory within the fertile soil of school literacy and watched to see what new meanings would grow.

For many of my students, memory was not simply obeisance to an idealized past. Often, the past was put into conversation with the present in order to deepen understanding and so that the students could envision a more secure future for themselves and their families. Celso told me that he did not want his family to worry about money anymore. "It's important to remember" the past, he once reminded me, "because it's what we have survived." One of the functions of Celso's original story was that it has sponsored new, perhaps more urgent, stories, ones addressing the negative dimensions of his family's diaspora experience. He has since poignantly discussed and written about his mother, who, in the time I have known her, has worked packing tomatoes, as a caretaker, and most recently, in a pencil factory. When schoolchildren have gone on field trips to the factory, the workers—mostly immigrants, mostly women—call out from beneath their protective masks and the deafening drone of the machinery, "Get your education, don't work here!" Often, Celso's mother got up at

4:00 a.m. and didn't come home until the late evening. Celso has expressed repeatedly his desire to get an education to give back to his family. "I don't want to see my mother tired anymore. That's why I want to go to college," he once told me.

There are still Filipinos/as working in canneries and fishing boats, in the fields, sweatshops, and factories and in minimum-wage service jobs. Many of my students were growing up in a context of poverty or near poverty, with class segregation, nativism, and occasionally violence impinging on their movements within and outside the neighborhood. Yet despite these constraints, the children adapted, drawing from transcultural resources—with love, with care—to restore history, language, and culture, reassembled fragments, like those of Walcott's vase, described at the beginning of this chapter.

NURTURING

From my students I have learned about the structures and dynamics that deepen inequality. Through their generosity and openness, I have been introduced to alternative accounts of social development, judgment, and capability. Celso's orientation to the world was shaped by a sense of obligation to others through self-sacrifice; participating in networks of reciprocity; codes of hospitality; and *bayanihan* work, which, roughly translated from Filipino, is a tradition of cooperation and community work.

Celso himself assumed new responsibilities after his father's death. Most important, he became a nurturer. He regularly cooked meals for the family and took care of his older sister, Tita, who has a cognitive disability. "I'm the only one who can perfectly understand her," he once told me, "because I listen carefully." Like several of my students, he collected remittances and items such as food, clothes, and medicine to send to his people abroad. Celso also acted as a cultural broker, advocating for his family's needs, which was necessary because of the prejudice his mother had experienced as a result of her perceived "foreigner" status. She once told me, "I can't speak; I'm not literate, so I'm glad Celso has an education to be social." Although Celso's mother did speak English and was literate in at least three languages, she perceived herself as lacking what academics might call the "linguistic capital" to effectively recruit support outside her immediate network of friends and family.

Consequently it was Celso who investigated programs for Tita, talked with community outreach people, and helped complete important family paperwork. He also regularly volunteered as an altar boy at his church. Moreover, he was my teacher. For example, once, in the neighborhood church, he explained what one might consider the "semiotics" of his mother's religious faith as she knelt in front of a statue feeling "Mary's sorrow," one hand "raised in adoration," the other hand holding Tita's.

I find myself romanticizing this type of communitarian ethos, nostalgic about a time—perhaps somewhere in my family history—when people acted more selflessly and were more nurturing toward others. At the same time, I want to be sober about the economic and social realities underlying such contemporary immigrant sensibilities. One of the more heart-rending ironies is that the amount of service and care that Celso bestowed upon others may have been less than the amount he received from adults. The sociologist Arlie Russel Hochschild (2000) notes that care itself is a scarce and devalued resource in our global economy (pp. 143–144). As women such as Celso's mother are forced to take on additional jobs as nannies for the wealthy, their children assume new roles in what sociologists call global care chains. Celso's mother labored to support family in both the United States and the Philippines. Because her work was so emotionally and physically taxing, it was inevitable that she would have less energy to direct toward her own children. These children, in turn, had to sustain the tenuous bonds of support by taking on new responsibilities, such as nurturing siblings, parents, and grandparents. Celso professed an unwavering dedication to his mother: "I tell her if she needs a doctor, I get her a doctor. If she needs her medicine, I get her medicine. If she needs a massage, she gets a massage. I'll do anything."

SCHOOLING

Unfortunately, these ways of orienting oneself often exist in contradistinction to the dominant ideology of schools, which is one of competition and individualism. Rather than supporting the children's social knowledge, it may attenuate already fragile bonds. The rhetoric of educational reform in California is an alarmist tale of urban student failure. Curricula are manufactured to homogenize learning experiences and rank children on a unilinear scale, threatening to further marginalize some of our most vulnerable students. Children are thought of as the locus of problems that have prescriptive solutions: the correct phonics program based on the latest "brain research." Increasingly, students are told to conform to conventions— irrespective of whether it fits their sense of themselves—because they have to adjust to a harsh reality that has asserted itself through power. Sometimes the students do what they have to do to get through school, just as my grandfather worked as a houseboy in order to survive, even if school does not speak to their identities or inform who they would like to become.

In sixth grade, Celso began struggling with several of his classes. I was told he was "lazy." However, when put in a position of powerlessness within the school, many students will focus on areas where they have more creative agency and imaginative authority. In elementary school this may mean helping family and going to church youth groups and volunteering as an altar boy. In middle or high school, it may involve spending time with peers and adopting a more oppositional stance toward formal education. I often worry that in the dominant narrative of assimilation, the ending is either accommodation at significant cultural loss, or opposition.

This is when the work of cultivating a community through collective memory becomes all the more urgent. It is not the result of prescriptive "community building" activities. Rather, community is formed through particular understandings of individual children, their unique experiences and cultural identities, and is manifested in the quotidian, imperfect dynamics of everyday classroom interaction. This makes it a fragile and incomplete project. It may be especially difficult in overcrowded, underresourced schools. My response to Celso's story about his father was just one moment in an ongoing effort to nurture and sustain an intellectual and affective connection. In the years in which I taught fifth grade, my classes usually had about 35 students, with their own unique stories, experiences, and sometimes difficult relationships with schooling. I always felt that I was spread incredibly thin in terms of time and energy. And often when I had established trust and rapport with an individual child, he or she might move because of redrawn district boundaries or the generally high mobility rate within a school serving many low-income and migrant students.

Still, I believe that the lives and possibilities of my students were complex and open ended, even when they were being positioned negatively in school. Celso continued to self-identify as a poet and, on his own, has produced a significant body of work. When he was no longer a member of my fifth-grade class, he returned to my classroom regularly both for tutoring and to tutor my new students in history, music, poetry, vocabulary, and algebra. Celso and I also visited a photography exhibition at the local museum on the Filipino/a American immigrant experience in town.

In an old shoebox my grandmother had given me, I found a picture of my grandfather playing stand-up base for a "Filipino swing band" in New York City. Although he never made it as actor, he did eventually become a musician, and his weekend gigs would supplement his regular wages enough to provide his children with food, even during the Depression. I remember my grandfather telling me how important music was in his life, providing both the satisfaction of pleasing an audience and the companionship of fellow band mates. He was also very proud of his membership in the local musician's union.

THE FILIPINO DREAMLAND ORCHESTRA
HOTEL ASTOR   AUG. 19, 1938

The performance stage was my grandfather's own "magical box," an alternative space where he might imaginatively transcend daily realities and both recover and assert some truth about himself that society had denied. Similarly, by looking through our own boxes of family memory, Celso and I began to reassemble our respective family stories and histories in order to construct more empowering identities for ourselves. For Celso, this process of recovery and creation may have informed his identity as a young person, a young Filipino, trying to negotiate the educational system and cope with life more generally. For me, it informed my own professional identity as a relatively new teacher trying to provide future generations with access to a quality education that respected who they were. When schools threaten to render the imagination vacuous through a mandated curriculum and the stresses of evaluation, I remind myself that there are always deeper reservoirs: secret boxes to be tapped into; cultural practices to be nurtured; inchoate feelings that, through dialogue, take shape and gain rhetorical force. There are also stories born of loss and trauma. Under the right intellectual and emotional conditions, they may proliferate outward, enabling students (and teachers) to rediscover and re-create their communities.

CHAPTER 3

Carmen's Unwritten Story

Failing Our Students with Remediation

Real education should consist of drawing the goodness and the best out of our own students. What better books can there be than the book of humanity?

—Cesar Chávez

M Y MAIN RESEARCH QUESTION was the following: What would happen if I invited children from immigrant and migrant backgrounds to read, write, and speak from their own experiences and the realities of their lives? One of my initial findings was that I had difficulty even posing this question. Because our school was officially designated "low performing," the teachers were under constant pressure to standardize curricula according to "scientifically based research." I was provided with at least four literacy programs to implement in my classroom. Since I was new to the district, I struggled to weigh instructional mandates against my own desire to co-construct with my students a literacy curriculum built around their own experiences. I tried to create the conditions that would provide the possibility for students to inquire into their own lives in school.

DISCOVERING CARMEN'S ROLES

I attempted to wrest the life story of Carmen, and her father, Marcos, from classroom obscurity and anonymity during my first year in California. My goal at the time was to encourage Carmen to engage in complex literacy engagements that combined her more immediate life-world experiences with school-based knowledge and instruction. On several occasions, Carmen began to write her family's migrant narrative, but the project was always deferred because of what seemed more pressing bureaucratic demands. Carmen spent many of her school hours in programs that emphasized teaching skills in a prescriptive and decontextualized manner, often at the expense of deeper meaning. This provided little time for Carmen to develop an academic identity based on her own rich experiences and full humanity, not on failure and being constantly "behind." Her substantial potential remained latent beneath daily stresses and the grind of remediation.

The school perceived Carmen as a "reluctant learner" in continual need of basic instruction. She was marked as being in the lowest quintile band of students, according to testing, and had "deficits" to be "remedied." At the same time, she presented herself to me as a vital member of a larger community. If Carmen was a *client* at school for the latest remedial programs, she was very much a *contributor* at home and in the neighborhood. She played an instrumental role in fulfilling domestic responsibilities such as cooking; cleaning; and caring for her father, grandmother, and neighbors. She had friends from a variety of backgrounds and often displayed empathy for their needs and vulnerabilities. Carmen was, in fact, the first to recognize that I was new to town and extended an invitation to a neighborhood function. I suggest that these two presentations of Carmen—as a reluctant learner and as a child adept at negotiating the dynamics of her social milieu and creating solidarity with others—existed in a hierarchical relationship. In school, the construction of the former constrained the creativity and development of the latter.

Carmen often appeared disengaged from the prescribed curriculum. During regular instructional hours, in an overcrowded room of 35 students, she rarely participated in discussions or completed required basal assignments. She was self-conscious about being pulled out for so-called intervention programs, which she believed were for the "dumb kids." If Carmen resisted the school- and district-sanctioned curriculum, this did not imply that she lacked intellectual curiosity or a commitment to her peers and teachers. Carmen was one of a number of students who arrived at school early to generously help me prepare for class. She would remind me of birthdays and gather books and work together for children who had to miss significant amounts of school because of their parents' transient work lives.

In addition to attending to various needs of our classroom, Carmen used the time to express her interest in and develop a sophisticated understanding of Filipino/a American history and culture. Before the school day began, we would have regular conversations about the colonization of the Philippines, the contributions of Filipino migrant laborers in California, and what it meant to be a member of a diaspora community, separated from others by geography yet connected by shared history, culture, and tradition. She would also tell me about her own life outside school and encourage me to talk to her father, Marcos, who had many similar interests.

CARMEN'S FATHER

I first met Marcos at a neighborhood basketball game; and we shared pictures and stories, including my own Filipino grandfather's migrant narrative, while Carmen was on the court. Marcos identified himself as mestizo (of mixed Filipino and European descent) and had spent a good part of his life performing migratory stoop labor in the vineyards throughout California, Oregon, and Washington State. He had to retire, following back problems, and now spent the majority of his time making customized lowriders from discarded car parts in his backyard.

I ate several evening meals (what Marcos called camp food, a cuisine developed in migrant labor camps) at their house, interviewing Marcos with Carmen about his memories of working in the fields and his involvement with the Agricultural Workers Organizing Committee (AWOC), a predominantly Filipino union led by Larry Itliong, and the National Farm Workers Association (NFWA), founded by Cesar Chávez. In the following excerpts from our interview, Marcos recalls the Delano strike against 33 grape growers, in which both Mexican and Filipino agricultural laborers protested low wages and poor working conditions. He also discusses his need for communion with fellow workers and his hopes for Carmen's future. I share Marcos's words because I believe that they provide insight into Carmen's encounters with schooling. They also suggest how the students' own family backgrounds can enrich curricular possibilities.

ON THE DELANO STRIKE

MARCOS: You want the story? Right there [pointing to literature by the Filipino American Historical Society]. This guy I was telling you about, my cousin, he was into history too.
We had strike in the morning and in the afternoon. This was roughly in the mid-60s with the Mexicans. Well, the strike started in Delano. For some reason there weren't as many Filipinos. There were more Spanish people because we were close to the border.
I can remember the Filipinos had to carry guns because the strikers had guns. It tells you all right there [pointing again to the literature]. When I experienced that, I quit. They had fake police officers. They were hired by the company. They didn't want the strikers to come to the camps. The strikers, they tried everything to get around the law to get to the workers, and the company had a hard time to get them out.

GERALD: Why did you get involved in the strike?

MARCOS: The strikers, they pay you to go on strike. They gave you gas and you got free food. That's about it. I remember it was my brother and four of us; we were getting so much—just about $50 a day. That's putting our money together. Fifty bucks a day, just hold signs and go out and yell.

GERALD: How did you feel about that, getting paid to strike?

MARCOS: It was all right, just as I said, it was an experience, and I could make more in the fields. The company, they raised the salary because at the time it wasn't by the hour, it was by contract, and the contract is per box.

GERALD: What made you get out?

MARCOS: What got me out of it, with Chávez, it was the close of the season and it was time for me to attend to the lettuce from Coachella, Phoenix, Bakersfield, Delano, and Lodi. Lodi was the last season.

GERALD: How big a need was there for a strike?

MARCOS: Well, people were complaining in the camps. They wanted benefits and that the companies in towns and cities had benefits but a lot of it went the wrong way.

ON THE NEED FOR SOLIDARITY

GERALD: You once told me that you had to separate from your fellow Pinoys [Filipinos]?

MARCOS: You couldn't choose who to work with. Maybe it was meant like that. I guess it was, because it happened. You have to go to the office and get an assignment and go to that camp. I missed my friends and the stories from the *manongs* (the older generation of Filipino workers). Like, they got hung for dating White women. That's how strict it was. I didn't know it myself but each time you go to a different camp you hear different stories.

ON MARCOS'S HOPE FOR CARMEN

MARCOS: I was born in Salinas. I grew up in town. Mom and Dad separated. I went with my dad. He was a farmer, but I didn't care for it because I hate to haul weeds. You get blisters all over your hands. Now Carmen, I try to stay on her about her work, but I try not to put too much pressure. She's already been through so much, and my only hope is that she can take care of herself when I'm gone.

When I first listened to the interview I was struck by how Marcos, who had participated in the Delano strikes, deferred to the official historical documents before his own personal experiences. It was as if his oral testimony needed to be legitimized by an authoritative written version. I also became self-conscious about my own (perhaps academic) desire to hear or formulate some kind of thesis about Filipino/as in California, how their role in the unions, for example, differed from that of the Chicano/as. I was pressing Marcos for some principled opinion on the necessity of the strikes when, instead, he relayed a story of survival that had more implied political or ideological content.

One interesting pattern that emerged from the interviews concerns what linguists call the location of agency in personal experience narratives (Fairclough, 2000). I think Marcos saw the world as having many constraints, with occasional opportunities to procure a modicum of security in limited contexts by getting along with people, creating solidarity, and participating in protest; the sum total of these seized opportunities constituting one's resourcefulness, creativity, and social grace. Marcos participated in the strikes because he had the opportunity to "hold signs and go out and yell." He left the strike "to attend to the lettuce." Things were meant to happen because they happened, and all one could really do was follow the seasons. And although these moments of opportunity and resistance were a salient theme in his narrative, many times things just "went the wrong way." This is very different from a conception of one's work being shaped to fit one's entitled trajectory. The creativity of Marcos, his work on lowriders, was relegated to a separate sphere that would not easily translate into economic or social empowerment. During my years in the neighborhood, I have met many individuals with deep passion and exceptional talent—in music, boxing, fine art, history, carpentry, mechanics, engineering—who cannot cobble together anything more than tenuously living day to day.

CARMEN'S UNWRITTEN STORY

It dawned on me that Carmen's school experiences were not too dissimilar from those of the individuals I met in the neighborhood. Tests, evaluations, and programs were constantly foisted upon her, and all too often, they went the wrong way and only seemed to prolong her suffering. It was as if the school was reproducing conditions of insecurity and expected failure that were, in some ways, parallel with the economic hardships that many of the neighborhood families endured. It was also one of the first times that I felt, at a gut level, Freire's (1970/1996) insight about how the education of the poor, with its deficit-based instruction, exploits this fatalistic sensibility by making poor students only receivers and victims of knowledge, not creators. And while the rhetoric of school has inculcated within Carmen the belief in a self-authorized life, the structure of schooling is conditioning her to accept her situation in life and to internalize a sense of failure.

I was pleased when Carmen decided she was going to write her father's biography and, in the process, create her own story anew. Her father made her a book cover (out of wood, hand carved, with a stylized map of the Philippines), to "safeguard their story," as he put it. Carmen and I listened to and discussed the transcripts of her father's interview. She began writing about his life in the context of everything else she was learning about Filipino/a American history. She said it was the most she had ever written in school. I was proud of Carmen when she stood in front of class, holding the cover, and announced that her father was a fieldworker, yes. But he was also a historian of Filipino America and an artist (he was the first mestizo whose work made the cover of *Lowrider Magazine*). She read the opening lines of her story to her peers:

> My father is a hero. He traveled up and down California as a
> fieldworker and to places like Washington State. He worked in
> Phoenix, Bakersfield, Delano, and Lodi. He also fought for the
> rights of migrant workers and even went on strike.

Carmen had previously been reluctant to read out loud. She told me that in first grade she had become "afraid to make mistakes." But on this day she read the opening of her father's biography with confidence and eloquence.

Unfortunately the story was never completed. I became absorbed with testing, evaluation, programs, and paperwork. I had five-paragraph essays to administer on mandated topics, such as "snacks." Carmen continued to get pulled out to get drilled on isolated skills. I never provided the adequate scaffolding to enable her to lift her story out of obscurity—the deeper, more meaningful, and more difficult work. Carmen's narrative could have also inspired a class inquiry into local history. We might have examined, for example, the braided histories of Mexican and Filipino laborers and how different ethnic groups cooperated to work toward a vision of social justice. The children's own familial stories could have become a curricular resource. But I had not fully developed a pedagogy that built on and developed the experiences and realities of the students' lives, a pedagogy based on the theoretical assumption that critical inquiry into these very experiences might yield genuine knowledge about what it means to teach and learn in diverse urban schools. I was not able to provide the opportunities for Carmen and others to translate their experiences into the contexts of schooling with pragmatic effects, enabling them to become agents in their own educational development. Carmen was subsequently subject to even more remedial "intervention" programs.

That summer, only weeks before sixth grade was to begin, Carmen received a letter stating that she would have to spend her final year of elementary education in another school because the district had redrawn its boundaries. Despite the talk in our district of the importance of creating a school community, she was removed from the community she had been a member of since kindergarten. Although this larger decision made sense to those on one level of the educational bureaucracy, it was experienced as arbitrary and cruel by Carmen, her father, and hundreds of other displaced children and their families, who were not involved in the decision-making process. Are the children just numbers to be reshuffled, many wondered? Would this happen in affluent districts? Or was this just another forced migration and another example of a population being crossed by a border?

SCHOOLING AS EXCLUSION

Several years later, Carmen came to visit me after school, as she had been doing intermittently. She told me, with sincere optimism, that she wasn't failing three of her classes, and she reinforced an abstract commitment to the value of getting a good education. I was pleased to hear that she had recently gone to a meeting of the local chapter of the Filipino American Historical Society on her own initiative; but I was disheartened to learn that her interest in her cultural roots was not being encouraged or developed within the context of her formal schooling. She gave me a video and some articles about Filipino American history from her father, "to keep," she said. He had "been wanting" to invite me to dinner again, to introduce me to his secret barbecue-sauce recipe, but he was in too much pain. He was dying of cancer. The doctor had given him at most 3 months to live. Carmen told me that if he passed away, she would continue to live with her aging grandmother. They would care for each other.

Without adequate health-care services, Carmen continued to nurture her father throughout the duration of his sickness and physical deterioration: "I was with him, like his personal nurse. I took care of him in our house, not the hospital. I was the only one with him while he was really hurt, until the very end. I heard his last words." When Carmen found out I was moving from California, she came to my classroom regularly at lunchtime to help me pack my teaching belongings. During one of her last visits, she gave me a leaflet in honor of her father that had been distributed at his funeral. It had a prayer inscribed on one side and a picture of Marcos on the other, depicting him proudly kneeling in front of a customized car he had built, holding a trophy that honored his talents.

Carmen missed a lot of school when she became her father's primary caretaker during the final months of his life. This served to compound her already low academic achievement and her own feelings of frustration. She had been retained twice, and, at 14, was embarrassed to still be in seventh grade at the neighborhood middle school. She began failing most of her classes and was developing an oppositional relationship with schooling.

Although Carmen said she liked many of her teachers, she nevertheless felt infantilized because they still made her sound out letters and words, "just like I was doing in first grade."

I worry that many children in situations similar to Carmen's will adjust their aspirations to conform to the expectations of a system that does not recognize their skills, intellect, creativity, and promise. This may occur suddenly; I have witnessed, for example, previously diligent fifth graders begin the sixth year by flouting school authority. More often, I have found, it transpires over time: a steady, not fully conscious disenchantment with what formal education has to offer, spirits ground down by tasks that seem to have no relevance to students' immediate lives, their potential contributions diluted by an ideology that equates material poverty with cultural deprivation. I also worry that school is preparing students like Carmen to assume low-wage positions in the service industry, whose work will be too isolating to create solidarity with others, the way her father bonded with those with whom he labored in the fields.

I hope Carmen's resourcefulness and social grace will be recognized as valuable. Carmen and I share the desire to find connections and create new meaning across boundaries of difference—quite the opposite, it seems, of the system's deficit-driven compulsion to dissect and categorize. Maybe this is the collaborative work of our diaspora.

THE SECOND CLASSROOM

I retell Carmen's story to account for and capture the complexity of those experiences that defy conventional ways of making sense of urban students. Carmen is a remarkable young person, but the regular academic curriculum has failed her. It did not draw on, as the Cesar Chávez quote suggests, her "goodness" and the "best" she had to offer. Out of school, she was a competent and invaluable contributor to friends and family. In school, she was positioned as a reluctant learner who was often considered defiant and immature. She was not provided with the opportunities to incorporate her rich cultural identity and life experiences into her formal schooling.

Carmen's story helped me identify the conflict between standardization and identity in our schools. It also pointed toward a possible resolution, affirming the need for teachers to cultivate multiple curricula that meet bureaucratic demands as well as the personal needs and capacities of our increasingly diverse student populations.

I realized that I had been teaching in two classrooms: a *first* mandated classroom and a *second* classroom that occurs during the margins and in between periods of the school day. In the first classroom are the time and energy spent on mandated tasks of which teachers are becoming all too familiar—basal instruction, testing, test preparation, and codified teaching strategies that focus on the transmission of discrete skills. The second classroom runs parallel to, and is sometimes in the shadow of, the official, first classroom. It is an alternative pedagogical space. It develops organically by following the students' leads, interests, desires, forms of cultural expression, and especially stories. It is part of regular instructional hours, but it also occurs before school, after school, during recess, during lunch, and occasionally on weekends and extends beyond the immediate classroom walls, into homes and community spaces. It also operates by a different sense of time, largely improvisational, aspiring to respond to opportunities creatively.

The second classroom is an ideological space as well. It is *second* because it is the work of the students and teachers that remains for the most part, invisible and uncompensated, both in terms of funding and recognition. It includes the relationships that they build and nurture with one another as they share their life stories. The second classroom also has an affective dimension, involving the emotional labor of teachers as they struggle to execute the mandated curriculum while nurturing the individual and cultural integrity of children. When I conducted the research for this book, I was not familiar with Third Space "hybrid literacy practices" (Gutierrez, Barquedano-Lopez, & Tejada, 1999; Gutierrez, Barquedano-Lopez, & Turner, 1999). My concept of the second classroom is compatible with this important work.

I suggest that I may have failed Carmen because the second classroom remained subordinate to the first. I needed to be more imaginative about providing opportunities for Carmen to contribute to her own education by bringing her rich life experiences into the literacy curriculum. I never adequately provided the requisite structures of support that might have privileged her particular set of cultural resources. Her identity became obscured by a standardized and overly rigid notion of educational worth and growth to which she did not measure up.

During my first year, Carmen, Marcos, and Celso helped me realize that the work done in the second classroom could become the very material from which to fashion curricula. The buried histories that our narratives materialize, the sense of community we establish through memory, the relationships we nurture and sustain, and the children's own life experiences would all become important intellectual and academic resources. These resources are similar to the "funds of knowledge" of "working-class minority students," which all too often are overlooked in favor of school-sanctioned, deficit-based instruction that homogenizes classrooms and lowers expectations (Gonzalez et al., 1995, p. 445). They reveal histories and experiences that are buried by the pressures of standardization and became the basis for an alternative curriculum.

This curriculum often drew on sources of identity and insight that exist outside the ambit of official school discourse and knowledge—experiences that may have never taken shape as classroom literacy, stories of servitude and work that are usually not told because they are too busy being lived. This curriculum attempted to sustain the rawness and poignancy of those painful moments of familial and cultural disjuncture so that they could be transformed and reassembled into new possibilities for the future.

Some of my most profound teaching moments occurred when our classroom literacy engagements became informed by the students' own experiences and identities. By finding a variety of ways in which to share their ethnic and migrant narratives, students participated in their own instruction and educational development. When this was done well, they performed at levels equal to or surpassing those of any peer group across the country, even by conventional measures such as standardized-test scores. But the idea of the second classroom I am proposing does not provide any easy resolutions. In a climate of remediation, standardization, and high-stakes testing, a teacher's ability to fulfill the needs of the school institution and accommodate the specific experiences and stories of students rests on his or her individual capacity to negotiate agendas that are often in direct conflict. Perhaps more than anything else, Carmen's narrative taught me to confront my own personal limitations as well as the pain of uncertainty and, at times, feelings of hopelessness related to being an urban educator. Until our profession is reoriented to more systematically and comprehensively support and develop the experiential knowledge of both students and teachers, I believe, children like Carmen will continue to fall through the cracks.

PART II

Literacy Practices in the "Second Classroom"

I N THE SECOND PART OF THE BOOK I explore the varied school literacy practices that emerged from the "second classroom." I begin by describing how writing can bring about personal transformation, then how individuals use writing to reach outward and connect to a larger world, and finally how the various identities of the class interact and come together through collective performances.

In Chapter 4, I describe how current notions of educational accountability may reinforce deficit views of students and communities. Chapter 4 is also about the negative discourse that schools sometimes engender: for example, notions that children are "lazy" and "defiant" or that their families "don't care" and "don't value education." This type of accusatory discourse plagues many students, and it eventually comes with a cost, including tracking, expulsion, and other forms of social stigmatization and exclusion. I attempt to demonstrate the students' abilities to display agency and resistance by "writing back" to stereotypical representations of their neighborhood and school.

In Chapter 5 I examine how autobiography becomes a means by which students work through trauma; in Chapter 6, the way students use writing to locate and articulate themselves as members of transnational communities; and in Chapter 7, how *teatro*, a form of political theater that has its roots in El Teatro Campesino, becomes a vehicle through which the children can assert both individual history and group solidarity.

CHAPTER 4

"We Are Strong and Sturdy in the Heart"

Redefining Accountability

> In all human relationships, and helping another is a form of relationship, we have to respect other persons. . . . We have to give what we have, but in order to do that we have to be attentive to what others experience as their needs.
> —Gustavo Gutierrez, *Sharing the Word Through the Liturgical Year*

WHAT DOES ACCOUNTABILITY MEAN to those who work daily in urban schools and communities? Are the only versions of accountability that are worth considering those that have fallen from the policy sky? Might teachers and students, through their relationships with one another, create their own versions of accountability? Or, perhaps most important, what are the preconditions for accountability? What types of research orientations, social arrangements, and practices might best enable us to learn about and adjudicate between competing educational values and outcomes?

One inroad into these questions is to consider two ways to think about the word *accountable*. In the current educational climate, the term has an obvious quantitative, policy-oriented valence: it implies "to quantify, to count, to measure costs and benefits." Through a high-stakes-testing and standardization paradigm, schools, teachers, and students are held accountable to the system, to politicians, to an abstract "public." People are reduced to numbers. For example, it is not uncommon for teachers to be disappointed when new students or returning migratory students arrive in school before "testing," because the teachers are concerned that such students might bring the scores down. A new member of the school community should be a cause for celebration, not frustration.

Yet the word *accountable* also has a qualitative, ethical valence. At more immediate local levels, teachers, students, family, and community members account for one another and are accountable to one another, not in an abstract moralizing sense that suppresses difference, conflict, and inequality—"no child left behind"—but through ethical practices that are attuned to and help us discern the complexity of situations. In this sense *to be accountable* means—at its simplest—to be mindful of engagement with others, to learn productively from and respond to the experiences of others, and to cultivate mutual empathy and understanding. It is about relationships.

I worry that increasingly the narrow political and instrumental sense of *accountability* undermines teaching as an ethical practice. In fact, the bureaucratic mechanisms that "hold schools accountable" may be partially accountable—as it were—for the very experiences that disenfranchise and stigmatize urban students. For example, norm-referenced tests create bell curves that correspond with class distinctions. All too often, these tests also inform educational decisions that deny children from low-income families the learning experiences that will prepare them for college, as they are kept from exposure to algebra, engagement in high-quality literature, and access to opportunities to cultivate their own critical perspectives. The pressures to teach to the test may divert attention away from the complexity and capacities of individual learners and perhaps may even drive the most creative and qualified professionals away from the most underresourced schools.

Accounting for others, therefore, entails much more than listening well or what is often coded as the soft interpersonal dynamics of teaching. It may involve working both within and against the system to discern what is best for students. It is academic and sometimes activist labor that should be articulated and systematically manifested in our theories of practice. Further, I believe that it involves recognizing our students' experiences and identities as reservoirs of knowledge and creating conditions for "epistemic cooperation" (Mohanty, 1997)—forms of collaborative ethical and political investigation that may enable us to critique unjust educational arrangements and dominant understandings in order to imagine and create other possibilities. This type of cooperation begins with respecting the local knowledge of the communities with whom we work.

RESIDENTIAL STIGMA

One pernicious stereotype about urban communities and schools is that of cultural and social deprivation. This is evident in everyday talk. I have been privy to far too many conversations, even in the teacher's lounge, in which children and their families are unfairly blamed. But this stereotype is also manifested in a number of educational practices, such as standardized remedial education, the elimination of bilingual programs, and approaches for working with poor children that suggest that they do not think as abstractly as their middle-class peers. In a prevailing mythology of urban teaching, the classroom is a site of mastery; the master teacher is the one who already knows what is best for students and micromanages every aspect of the content, time, and physical space of the school day. Through a distanced and supposedly objective educational gaze, children and schools are evaluated by means of criteria formed by impersonal and consequently mystifying bureaucratic processes. What occurs beyond the walls of the class, the myth implies, is the absence of structure and predictability. It may not be too far a stretch to liken the teacher in this context to a Crusoe figure, building a refuge of order in a beleaguered and chaotic urban environment.

An article in the local paper describes the school neighborhood in which I taught as being the most segregated from the town's population of non-Hispanic Whites. As in many cities and towns, segregation has become a correlate for poverty, crime, and supposed cultural deprivation. This perception is reinforced in the article, which quotes a man who "is not too interested" in venturing south of Cesar Chávez Avenue, one dividing line, after dark. The article goes on to delineate the city's neighborhoods:

> In another south side neighborhood, Gloria and Martha can't ignore the clear division between their part of town and the north side. The Filipina teenagers live near the Interstate, just south of Cesar Chávez Ave.
>
> When they run into teens from the north side, at the mall or at football games, they hear: "You're from the south side. You're ghetto."

Many of my students seemed inured to such stereotypes. They were topics of everyday conversation and were an unyielding feature of the city's cultural geography. These stereotypes were implied in a cultural tour of the city that skirted one of the most historic Filipino neighborhoods in the country; woven into the ideology of a nearby teacher education program that dissuaded its students from apprenticing in the city schools, channeling them to more affluent districts; obvious in the injunction to teachers not to make home visits on their own; replayed when taking a basketball on an elementary school yard escalated into a police intervention; and branded into the consciousness of a second grader who was accused of stealing a new Hello Kitty wallet, which was given to him as a gift—the racial profiling of a six-year-old.

But as the Chicana author Sandra Cisneros makes clear, there are other forms of knowledge that are generated from the intricacies and intimacies of shared space. In *The House on Mango Street* (1987) she decenters the all-knowing or controlling narrator in an ensemble of vignettes that weave a variety of voices to create a collective neighborhood representation. In the passage below the young speaker's nuance of judgment is based on relationships, an understanding of personal eccentricity, and family history. This type of insider knowledge is contrasted with the narrow perspective of those who come into the neighborhood, roll up their windows and look straight ahead, the irony, of course, being the ease with which people lapse into similar prejudices once rolls/roles are reversed:

> Those who don't know any better come into our neighborhood scared. They think we are dangerous. They think we will attack them with shiny knives. They are stupid people who are lost and got there by mistake. But we aren't afraid. We know the guy with the crooked eye is Davey the Baby's brother, and the tall one next to him in the straw brim, that's Rosa's Eddie V., and the big one that looks like a dumb grown man, he's Fat Boy, though he's not fat anymore nor a boy.
>
> All brown all around, we are safe. But watch us drive into a neighborhood of a different color and our knees go shakity-shake and our car windows get rolled up tight and our eyes look straight. Yeah. That is how it goes and goes. (p. 28)

Urban teachers potentially assume professional identities analogous to these fearful outsiders. We carry the freight of our educational training, focus on our objectives, and shut out anything that may threaten our sense of authority or security. Our students are often seen obliquely, as clients for the latest programs.

THE NEIGHBORHOOD WRITES BACK

For some students, educational and social mobility may hinge on the ability to distance themselves from the neighborhood, their success fueled by shame. I worry that children may adjust their aspirations to conform to the expectations of "those who don't know"—don't know their skills, creativity, and promise. However, provided a forum, students may "write back" to stereotypical images of their communities. In order to counteract negative preconceptions of the neighborhood that influence educational policy and that the students might be liable to internalize, I employed stories from *The House on Mango Street*, which offers a literary model of an analogous neighborhood.

Cisneros's story "Those Who Don't Know" served as one pedagogical cue, a way to signal to the students the importance of their own local knowledge. In the following examples, Simon and Maria respond in writing to the story. Both students challenged distorted representations from the social location of the neighborhood itself. Their own autobiographical writing became a vehicle for them to critically mediate their understandings of the neighborhood, resist preconceptions, and analyze the material conditions that threatened to diminish their life opportunities. In this instance, our research in the second classroom, described earlier, extended into the community. The students cited their own local observations and experiences as a reliable source. The first piece is Simon's, and Maria's follows:

> My neighborhood is multicultural. It has mostly Filipinos, Mexicans, and black people—like a trilogy of cultures. Everybody gets along around my part of the neighborhood, but the other part can be a living nightmare. In the enraged part, people have shallow friendships. They are eager to fight, talk coarsely, act belligerently. I love my part of the neighborhood because people have intense friendships.
>
> The advantage of a diverse neighborhood is when you get along with other cultures, the violence diminishes. I would love to learn a surplus of things from different people. For example, you may learn different languages and abilities. You can be a philosopher and answer unanswered questions like how to become a pacifist and help people stop violence.
>
> The problem in our neighborhood is too many people go to jail. I want a city filled with extraordinary minds. The people who go to jail make wrong choices because someone treated them without respect, or they didn't get many compliments to encourage them. We should stop making criminals, but we should make intelligent people by giving youth an education. Minorities should be treated with the same respect as people in the majority. Just because they have color does not mean that they are not smart. As Martin Luther King said, "Judge people not by the color of their skin, but by the content of their character." It's not the skin color that counts, but the heart and brain. (Simon, "the poet," fifth grade, 10 years old)

> Most outsiders have stereotypes about South Side for some reason. They think we are ignorant. My perspective is just to ignore the rubbish they say. I went to a North Side school and I was the only Filipino attending. I wanted to go back to my neighborhood school because we are very diverse. We have Lao, Pakistani, Chinese, Hmong, Filipino, Mexican, and African American students. South Side has been my home for ten years and I hope it will be my home

for many more. Remember, we may have dilapidated buildings, but we are strong and sturdy "in the heart." This is my message to the world. (Maria, fifth grade, 10 years old)

Both Maria's and Simon's responses indicate that the problems in the neighborhood are more than merely statistical. Resources are scarce; jobs, schools, livable wages, and access to health-care services are hard to come by. There are children with incarcerated family members. The students themselves are unsentimental about conflicts they have witnessed.

However, Simon's critical insight is that many of the conditions of his neighborhood are the results of social processes that originate outside the neighborhood. He indicts a society that "creates criminals" and does not treat "people in the minority" with respect. In her response, Maria strives to reclaim the neighborhood in terms of her own experiences. She writes authoritatively of the disparity between etic and emic perspectives. Like Simon, she is concerned about the ways in which outsiders conflate poverty with ignorance. Following the passage quoted above, her essay goes on to describe the school's many accomplishments, including success in the academic pentathlon.

Even conflict and challenge may become part of a counter knowledge base. Both Simon and Maria recognize that the neighborhood's strength lies in its diversity. Maria asserts the value of going to school with "Lao, Pakistani, Chinese, Hmong, Filipino, Mexican, and African American students." Part of having access to a quality education involves learning with and from others. As Simon makes clear, the intermingling of ethnic and class sensibilities is a generative condition for intellectual and ethical investigation. Simon would eventually research and write about inequality in the criminal justice system and create a book of poetry, inspired by Langston Hughes, about his neighborhood.

At the end of her response to Cisneros, Maria alludes to a class discussion we had about the title of Carlos Bulosan's novel (1946/1973) *America Is in the Heart*. I had shared the story with the class of how my grandfather, a contemporary of Bulosan, considered himself an American long before he even left his small village in Mindanao. For my grandfather, as for Bulosan, the United States was not the property of a specific group, but the property of the "heart," of the imagination. Maria would extend this legacy by writing about her identity not simply as that of an American and a Pinay from the south side of town, but also as that of a critic of American imperialism (she wrote a piece of historical fiction about the Philippine-American War inspired by family stories) and member of a greater transnational community who envisions more universalistic responsibilities toward the poor of the world.

As I reviewed and strived to respond to the work of my students, I realized that they were not merely resisting distorted representations of their neighborhood and critiquing unjust social arrangements; they also drew on their own critically literate legacies—the work of Dr. Martin Luther King Jr., Carlos Bulosan, Sandra Cisneros, Jose Rizal, Dolores Huerta, and the Teatro Campesino—and most important, on their own experiences, in order to educate "those who don't know" about the world and how it affects them.

CHAPTER 5

"I Will Tell You a Little Bit About My People"

Narrating Immigrant Pasts

Long before children have any acquaintance with the idea of nation, or even of one specific religion, they know hunger and loneliness. Long before they have encountered patriotism, they have probably encountered death. Long before ideology interferes, they know something of humanity.
—Martha Nussbaum, in *For Love of Country*

WHAT WOULD IT MEAN TO CONCEIVE the classroom as a space in which students are invited to craft narratives out of their family's diaspora and refugee experiences? This chapter is about the role that storytelling and listening can play with students from families and communities that have endured uprooting, loss, and suffering. My decision to employ the migrant and refugee experience in the classroom is based on my observations, noted previously, that many students who have been negatively labeled or accused of being lazy, disrespectful, or confrontational are in fact often coping with issues such as poverty, memories of war and flight, the death of loved ones, the incarceration of family members, racism, and the ongoing challenges of crossing political borders and cultural boundaries.

Providing opportunities for students to narrate some of the more difficult aspects of their lives may serve a number of important purposes. Storytelling is one way in which students can begin to understand and perhaps gain a degree of control over past experiences that may not have been fully intelligible at the time of their occurrence. Stories serve an immediate, pragmatic goal: The students may use family and group history and collective memory as an academic resource. Events of the past are given new meanings in new educational contexts. Through storytelling the students are able to examine their own current lives—including their lives in school—take intellectual and ethical stands, and make their unique voices audible to wider audiences in a manner that may feel personally authentic while at the same time enabling them to negotiate academic expectations.

NECESSARY SILENCES

Erica Lee, a friend and colleague, shared with me the following vignettes about her mother, Karen, which she learned about in an interview she conducted with Karen:

> My mother's earliest memory from China is of hiding in the bushes from Japanese soldiers. Her mother was covering her mouth so they wouldn't be heard. That was her earliest and only memory of her biological mother. She was then given to a woman whom I call my grandmother. This woman also put her in someone else's care when she immigrated to the States. She sent money back, which was supposed to pay for my mother's education. Instead, the woman kept the money and put my mother to work like a child servant or slave.

Karen's story invokes a powerful image of the irreducibility of the traumatic experience and its resistance to articulation and sense making. The child's cries are muted by the mother's hand. Not having a voice is, in this case, literal. Silence is a tactic of survival under conditions of immediate threat. At the same time, there are no words to describe a child's intimation of death and subsequent abandonment, of being twice orphaned.

Many of our students have endured significant loss in their lives outside school. As in Karen's story, sometimes the immediacy of our students' experiences may be overwhelming and defy complete coherence and communicability. Marvin witnessed his father's murder when he was only 4, on a public street, giving him a memory he carried with him to five different elementary schools. Ma-Lee lost a sibling to malnutrition in Laos. Kari remembered hunger. AJ's biological father was in prison. Umberto's uncle was shot in the park. Flora, in response to a chapter from *Harry Potter*, wrote the following about the Mirror of Erised, an item in the book that reflects one's greatest desire:

> If I could look in the Mirror of Erised, I would see my cousin who passed away. He was funny, sensitive, smart and cool. He died from a gang. This part was sad in his funeral. When they started to bury him in his coffin, his mother fainted.

The children told of these experiences casually, almost as if they were reporting a bit of information they had heard about someone else. More often, the experiences were bracketed within daily conversation, an assumed, commonplace reality. The image of Karen and her mother in hiding, mouths covered, awakens us to countless other necessary silences in a classroom of immigrants, migrants, and refugee children. It calls into question our ability to ever really know our students, what they have been through, and their understandings of value and success. These are children who may have been "possessed," as Caruth (1996) would say, by their histories.

SILENCING IN SCHOOLS

In a classroom of children from immigrant, migrant, and refugee families, there may be practical as well as profound psychological and historical factors that trouble our ability to know our students. Yet the school's attempt to know them, or to assimilate their varied backgrounds into bureaucratic categories and prescriptive curricula may, in fact, exacerbate their predicament.

One bureaucratic response to students who have lived through difficult episodes in their lives is to treat them as objects of correction and remediation. It is less costly to blame students than to provide them with adequate resources. It is easier to implement prescribed curricula to "remedy" individual problems than to create the intellectual, emotional, and affective conditions that enable students to draw on their own cultural resources in order to fully realize their full academic potential. One of the greatest challenges of urban teaching is to not let systemic inequalities— racism, overcrowded and otherwise poor teaching conditions, punitive approaches to working with children—become normalized.

One cause of silence is the asymmetrical power dynamics between the school and the community. Can there be genuine and open conversation when children feel vulnerable to authority? I think of Carlos, a student who refused to share his family's story out of fear of disclosing information that might lead to his father's deportation; of Jasmine, who missed class for weeks on end, partially because she thought the school officer would take her from her grandmother. Then there were many other families who had— at one time or another—engaged the school, deferred to its authority, only to find out that doing so wasn't in their child's best interest. Hugh Mehan (1996) has demonstrated how learning disabled (LD) students become "objects," represented primarily as texts, as they move from "the classroom to testing to meeting rooms," where a "technical, quasi-scientific" psychological discourse trumps the more narrative and contextual insights of parents and teachers (pp. 271–272). Children are thus labeled. Without the means to challenge these "institutionally sanctioned identities" parents often maintain a low profile. One father confided to me:

> We didn't think our son was learning disabled, but we didn't know how to argue against numbers. Now he believes he is stupid. If we have to go to meetings, we smile and omit our thoughts, but the nurturing takes place at home.

Pierre Bourdieu (1993) describes a world where "a multiplicity of co-existing, and sometimes directly competing, points of view" produces new kinds of social suffering (p. 3). I believe that urban educators encounter and participate in this reality with particular poignancy. The school is at the nexus of histories, where continents merge and people come together in communities convulsed by economic and demographic shifts that deepen inequality. Classrooms are often small and crammed with bodies. But that is only one part of the challenge. Teachers find themselves faced not only with 35 children, but also with children who come from a wide range of cultural and linguistic backgrounds. The challenge for a researcher is equally daunting: to formulate manageable research in a social situation that is inherently unstable. On several occasions, I developed the requisite trust and rapport with families for teaching and qualitative research, only to have the children move or be removed from the school.

FROM SILENCE TO VOICE

The story of Karen and her mother in hiding, passed down to her daughter Erica in the context of a college assignment, is also part of a larger story, the unfolding of Karen's life and that of her family. It is situated within a constellation of experiences, including not only childhood exploitation in China, but also the fate of Karen's life as an economic refugee in the United States: the xenophobia, language difference, continued gender discrimination, and lifelong work in a cannery. It is about yoking together two cultures to create additional roles for herself and a supportive environment for her children and family.

The work of Caruth (1996) is instructive in this matter. She reminds us that trauma is not simply located at a specific moment in time; instead it is characterized by "belatedness" (p. 4). Since the actual force of the traumatic episode initially subverts interpretive frameworks, its meaning is often constituted retroactively in "different times and places" and also by different people in those places. The temporal component has implications for the way in which intergenerational knowledge is negotiated.

In contrast to simple cultural transmission or conflict, migrant children engage dialectically with the living past. Vivian Gadsden (1992) defines a phenomenon that she calls "literacy as legacy," in which what is passed on to future generations are "the multiple strands of meaning, and the expectation that literacy will help them expand meaning into meaningfulness in the varied contexts in which they learn and grow" (p. 335).

Often, immigrant, migrant, and refugee children bear witness to their parents', as well as their own, suffering. It is difficult to isolate hardship in any individual psyche; it spills, so to speak, onto the fabric of the diaspora. A child, being at once removed and part of what his or her family has endured, may be in a unique position to make new sense out of what has happened. The passage from silence to voice may be achieved through intergenerational storytelling.

"Hearing my mom's story," Erica concluded, "has given me a deeper appreciation of who my students are and made me rethink my roles and responsibilities to the community." Parents who are of the working poor may become increasingly insulated as they are preoccupied by the daily tasks of providing the basic necessities of life. They may look to their children as being extensions to a world that is foreign and at times hostile. Success in their own sphere—survival—may authorize them to endorse their children's entry and success in new spheres, such as school and community activism.

INTERGENERATIONAL STORYTELLING

The students' success therefore may involve a revisiting, rather than a repressing, of collective memory. Rather than be passive receivers of history, the students may draw on group experience in order to give new intellectual and ethical resonance to their lives. One child, Ada, wrote the following poem, titled "Abuelita" (Grandmother), inspired by Luis Villobos's "Tio Juancho" in June Jordan's (1995) *Poetry for the People*.

ABUELITA

Agárrame de la mano [Hold my hand]
Take me to Durango
Mexico
Let me see the way your *vida* [life] was
Take me and hold me close
Show me the ways of Mexico

Show me what *abuelito* [Grandfather] was like
Where he worked
And if you still said "Ay Senor" when you got mad
Show me your home,
Your "Casa de Dinero" you called it,
Show me, show me
Show me the ways you cooked *chile colorado y gorditas*
All the tasty stuff
Take me to your friends,
Show me when my aunts and uncles shared
Only one room in the house
Show me *abuelito* when he came home
With only three small pesos and how hard it was
For you, *abuelito* and my aunts and uncles
And most of all show me you,
When you were young,
Show me,
Show me.

In the poem, Ada expresses an urgency to know, to have revealed for her, her own family history, potentially imbuing her own education with a sense of intellectual and ethical focus.

Ada also eloquently captured the challenges of her own life in an analogy to a passage from Salman Rushdie's (1991) fable *Haroun and the Sea of Stories*, which likens storytelling to juggling. The passage reads:

> Haroun often thought of his father as a Juggler, because his stories were really lots of different tales juggled together, and Rashid kept them going in a sort of dizzy whirl, and never made a mistake. (p. 16)

"I'm like Rashid," Ada suggested in our literature circle, "I am trying to juggle my Mexican culture, my American culture, my work in school, and my work at home. The only difference is that I make mistakes."

Other children were aware of their family's continued sacrifices. One child, KP, described his family's current migrant work:

> My dad and mom work in Alaska. Mom folds clothes and washes dishes. She works almost twenty hours a day. She is tired. I send candy and sometimes medicine. She gets paid $3,000.00. My dad is a fisherman. He catches four or five fish a day. After that he sorts out the fish, king crabs, and octopus. Sometimes when he has nothing to do he goes fishing so they have something to eat.

After working sometimes they go bowling or singing Karaoke. Sometimes they sleep four hours and go back to work. One time they returned home to California. They woke me up and said "We're here!"

Another student, Leticia, wrote a response to Langston Hughes's (1994) "Mother to Son":

DAUGHTER TO MOTHER

Mom I know you work hard and you work to feed me
I remember that you told me that you have to walk on your knees
and scrub the floor
Your boss would treat you like a slave
Your back hurts, your knees hurt, your hands hurt
And your heart hurts
I want to help you get an easy life
You emigrated from Mexico
When you were small you had no papers and no home in America
You worked in the fields in the hot sun
Sweat would come down your back
Then again your back, hands, knees, heart and your soul hurts
Dollars a day
I love you mom because you did the hardest thing that a child
        shouldn't do
I wouldn't be here if it weren't for you

Leticia's writing is about how an unjust economic arrangement—getting paid only dollars a day and being treated like a slave all for the lack of papers—becomes inscribed onto the bodies and experiences of poor workers. Similar to KP's story, Leticia's poem emphasizes her mother's physical and emotional exhaustion. Leticia herself had worked in the fields, and her poem echoes the cadence of that labor. When she performed the piece in class, she stressed the lines that refer to her mother's hurt and then paused slightly after the phrase "dollars a day," highlighting the injustice of the situation. And with an awareness of her mother's sacrifices comes a sense of responsibility: "I want to help you get an easy life."

Leticia's concern for her own family's experiences would eventually translate into a commitment to migrant families more generally. She researched the history of the United Farm Workers of America, specifically the life of Dolores Huerta, who was a family friend of one student in the class. Leticia even attended a rally for more expansive health care, sponsored by an interfaith community organization.

Leticia consistently expressed a concern for others in her writing, even in her more imaginative pieces. For example, inspired by a lesson on William Blake's "The Tyger," Leticia wrote the following poem about the legend of Llorona, a weeping spirit who roams the earth in search of her own children, whom she had drowned in a river:

LLORONA WHY?

Llorona Llorona why do you cry?
Is it because your children died?
You killed them it's your fault.
Just don't go out into the village
And scare people with your dreadful eyes.
Look for them in the sea,
Look for them some more,
If you don't find them,
Today's children you can adore.

Leticia told me that the message of the poem is that there are many children today that need attention and adoration. The students' writings and interests often indicated alternative sources of value that privileged cooperation and collective well-being.

NARRATIVES OF SURVIVAL

Instead of framing our students' lives by preordained categories of deficit, we might listen to the theories they have themselves developed by reflecting on the concrete realities of their own lives. It is through understanding the experiences of those most vulnerable, in this case girls from migrant and refugee families, that we may be best positioned to understand the complexities of urban teaching and learning.

Send me word like music Grandma
Take me back to our land, the land I was born in
Show me the works of the Philippines
Show me how to stay in business
Tell me how it feels selling fish in the market
And getting your back broken
Tell me the smell of fish while they're still fresh and watery
Show me the house you built with cardboard, metal, and sticks
Tell me the memories you remember so I can remember
(Priscilla, 10 years old)

I do not interpret the narratives of Priscilla and Ma-Lee that follow as simply mirroring an empirical past or fulfilling a classroom assignment that meets preset objectives. I read them more as acts of agency that refer to certain realities in their lives, while at the same time pointing toward a better world informed by a greater spiritual or cultural matrix that is not contained by the daily facts of existence. They may "shape action" as well as "contribute to the reality of their participants" (Rosaldo, 1989, p. 129).

The promise of the classroom may be to provide a respite for children to allow them to gain insight into their experience, and to allow opportunities for creating meaning out of potentially numbing contingencies. Priscilla's poem speaks of "words like music" from her grandmother and attends to her physical pain, her "back broken." As described in Chapter 2, Celso opened his father's secret box. In her autobiography, Ma-Lee, as we shall see, yearns for a world that is "radiant" and never "dim with prejudice." Children's writing as agency does more than just reflect their worlds; it is also pragmatic, transforming the world, at least the world of the classroom, if only modestly.

The survival stories, often born out of the "open wound of the border" (Anzaldúa, 1987), accomplish this by disrupting the boundary between public classroom discourse and the more private stories of families and community. The official point of entry for "the personal" is usually through the counselor's door, where professionals "diagnose" the children's needs, "prescribe" the necessary interventions, and counsel parents. Not considered a factor in official school knowledge, ethnicity is domesticated to an insular familial sphere, or staged as entertainment. The stories of Priscilla and Ma-Lee emerged from our classroom in highly mediated ways, reflecting the pragmatic concerns of the students themselves. They complicate notions of the confessional form, if a confessional mode is characterized by direct access to some kind of individual, psychological truth. As the literary critic Wendy Hesford (1999) argues, "The personal voice can be achieved apart from the individual's participation in social-material realities" (p. 56). The stories may be personal, but the emotions they convey have social import, reflecting readings of the world that are embedded in collective history and group experience.

Priscilla's Biography: "Not Me But Me"

Priscilla was a student in my class during my first year of teaching in California. The facts that I know of her life outside the school are few. She emigrated from the Philippines as a child. She has lived in a number of different homes in her young life, at times staying with relatives in a low-income housing project and in a homeless shelter, where "they gave us beds and extra clothes and on holidays treats." Priscilla wrote fondly of an African American woman who eased her family's transition to the neighborhood:

> At the shelter, there is one person I would really like to thank because she helped us get to where we are now, she was like a mom to us. Grandma Penny was a special, caring, and gorgeous female. We prayed for each other. My whole family felt really bad because she died of cancer. My mom didn't let us go to the funeral because it was too painful.

Both Priscilla's parents had several jobs, among them selling household items at the local flea market. Priscilla herself often spent her weekends at work or caring for her younger siblings while her parents labored in evening shifts. Over the summer she received a letter from the district informing her that she had to move to a new school. I have not seen her since, though children who frequented the flea market regularly told me she still lived in the neighborhood but had moved to another home.

During our collaborative inquiry into immigration, Priscilla wrote the following essay, titled "Biography of a Filipina Girl":

> In the Philippines there is mostly water because it is an island. Many people would think that it's easy to make money there, but they'd have to guess again. Hi! My name is Priscilla and I'm going to tell you what it's like being a Filipino girl.
>
> As everyone knows, whenever a baby boy or girl is born they'll have to be healthy, so that when they grow up they're a big help. A baby girl is now born and grows up to be thirteen years old, and is now working for money. The only job a girl like her could get is selling "sampagita" in the street, and would barely get like fifty cents from doing all that work. The only food that she might get to buy is fish because the whole salt lake is filled with fish. If they do not have any money left they'll take the last piece of fish, smell it, and eat rice.
>
> On holidays some Filipino girls put candles in glass on their heads. They also hold one on each hand, and while holding the candles someone else beats with two sticks and the girls have to dance. While the entertainment is being watched everyone eats and enjoys.
>
> Everyone needs to pay to get an education. It costs a lot to learn at school, but mostly every girl drops out just to help their parents because most parents get sick or fired from their work. The Filipina girl in the story is named Marilyn Reyes. She has now finished school and is working at the age of eleven in an ironing and washing job. That job was the only job that her and her mother could do, but as for

the dad, he is a standby who wants for someone to give him money in the street. That's how their life was: they never had a radio, TV, or even a refrigerator. They never got to buy those things with the money they were making by going to people's houses, picking up dirty clothes, and washing them. Marilyn and her mom's nightly work was selling "sampagita." That is where they are now.

Priscilla's biography is of a child she described as "not me but me." Priscilla created a composite portrait, one that is at once about an individual and a self that is representative of the lives of many. The hardships endured by Marilyn could have easily been features of Priscilla's own life's trajectory, or of that of any other girl from the same regional and class background in the Philippines.

Priscilla culled material from her own experiences and observations, as well as those of family and friends, to put forth what may be considered the other side of the conventional immigrant narrative of upward mobility: the story of those left behind. Marilyn is part of a permanent underclass—"that is where they are now," essentially where they have always been. Priscilla had, at the very least, an incipient understanding of the injustice of the situation. No matter the quantity of other people's "dirty clothes" they picked up and washed, they still couldn't afford the most rudimentary household items. In the story Marilyn represents herself and her people with dignity, honoring their work while at the same time, in the luminous third paragraph, about the candles of celebration, recognizing a cultural preserve, a moment of respite, from the ceaseless tasks of survival.

In some ways, Priscilla could have been considered a paradigm in her having what Ogbu calls the "dual frame of reference" accredited to "voluntary minorities" (Ogbu & Simons, 1998). No matter how difficult things become in the host country, it could be worse back in the place of origin. Priscilla goes on to write:

> America is full of opportunities, and you can't get homeless because there is shelter. Every person can afford to go to school. The Filipina girl in the story needs to wash clothes by hands, but in America they use washing and drying machines.

What is clear is that an alternative notion of childhood, responsibility, and value structured her interactions at home and in the neighborhood, something we could call a migrant ethos. It is characterized by a notion of a self that is intimately bound to others, in an interpersonal coordination of opportunity and response that, remarkably, can sustain a family as it continuously adapts to new environments.

When children such as Priscilla and Celso interacted with their families, they assumed a flexible and improvisational set of roles to accomplish simply what needed to get done, almost seamlessly moving between very different tasks. Priscilla also did well in school. She maintained an A average, had high scores on standardized tests, and continued to craft thoughtful and poignant essays. I attribute Priscilla's educational success to this ethos (her success was not the result of any consistency of curriculum: She has attended too many schools). Priscilla reminded me of how deep affective connections, even—maybe especially—across boundaries, facilitate the learning process: "I learned to speak English well because I loved to speak to Grandma Penny." These types of affiliations enabled her to create a home out of a state of homelessness, coherence out of a potentially fractured social reality.

Yet Priscilla's present life was strikingly similar to that of Marilyn. In her class journal, Priscilla wrote of weekends spent helping her mother at her work, helping her father at his work, caring for siblings, setting up the booth at the flea market, and helping her older sister at work:

1/19/99

On Friday I watched television and I also helped clean the house. In the morning my dad, mom, and big sister went to work, my sister left to help my dad at work, so I had to cook breakfast for my brothers. At night around 6 o'clock my dad and sister came home, and dinner was ready for them. We all watched a little more TV, but when it was 10 we had to go to sleep. I didn't go to sleep because I wait for my mom to come home [at] midnight, and then we went to sleep.

On Saturday my dad went to work extra time. . . . I went to the flea market to buy Mixtos ingredients. We went around the flea market thirty minutes or more looking for toys, books, and clothes. When we got home we started on the food so that when my dad got home we could eat. 3 minutes after 1 my mom got ready to go to work and my big sister also got dressed to go with my dad to work. Then again I was left home with my brothers, in charge and responsible until my dad and big sister came home. I also did my homework with a little help from my big sister, and we did some more things until the day was over.

The next day was Sunday which is a busy day for everyone in the family because we sell at the flea market, but we usually sell on

Saturday and Sunday except we had a break on Saturday. My big brother is in charge of loading our stuff inside the van, and my little brother doesn't do that much stuff because he is still too little to carry stuff around. My sister and I are in charge of setting the stuff on the table or either unpacking. My dad unloads the stuff, sets the tables, puts the tarp up, and also drives us there. We stayed there from 9 am to 5pm. Then my sister and I packed up, folded the covers on the table, and helped lock the tables up. When we got home, my big brother unloaded the stuff. My mom wasn't with us because she had to go to work at noon. We spent the rest of the day relaxed because we were all weary and lethargic.

Although her family was certainly wealthier in absolute economic terms than they had been in the Philippines, they were still struggling, and their poverty could be exacerbated by their new minority status. Forms of cultural capital they brought with them did not necessarily translate to new contexts; as newcomers, they were subject to distinctively American forms of exclusion and stigmatization. Many of my students endured race- and class-based prejudice and the daily stresses of just getting by. Priscilla herself was not a voluntary migrant to the United States: "My parents decided to come here, not me. I was just a baby!" It may be more accurate to say that students such as Priscilla are occupying new social positions and have access to multiple frames of reference as they find their place and make new space in the internal hierarchies of a segregated California barrio. That is, despite their hybridized identities, multiple social competencies, and ability to code-switch, they continue to face the obstacles of their class status.

I assume that Priscilla is currently preparing to enter high school. Unable to predict what is in store in her future, I am left with questions and hopes. I want her to invent her own world, one in which she sustains the valuable quotidian sensibilities necessary for community without perpetuating compulsory domestic and economic gender roles. I hope she continues to do well in school without compromising culturally based values and practices. But I am afraid that what is at stake are two models of childhood social and educational development that are fundamentally at odds. One of those is an ethic in which value is measured qualitatively and in relationship to others; the other is the dominant school ideology, which endorses an individualistic notion of the self—whose progress can be charted quantitatively through test scores and whose success is measured by conformity with or deviation from a norm.

This will be Priscilla's complex cultural work as she continually juggles the tensions and possibilities of the social spaces of her home, school, and peer group. I do not believe that such work can be theorized a priori by researchers and social scientists. There are too many unexpected complexities. This work is Priscilla's ongoing social reality, fraught with social and economic contingencies. As Priscilla steadily slips into my memory, she becomes part of a reservoir of experiences that I hope to transform into knowledge that will enable me to better prepare for and respond to a new group of 30 children with their own signature stories. But the truth is that I will never feel as though I can do my job adequately. Perhaps, at best, I can take my cue from Grandma Penny and aspire to have the class be just one node in a fragile network of support, one through which the children can obtain the emotional and intellectual resources to create new frameworks of meaning and possibility.

Ma-Lee's Story of Migration: "I Want to Be Part of Both Cultures"

Ma-Lee was initially introduced to me as a student with low standardized-test scores, in the lowest quintile for reading, and therefore as a child in need of some form of remedial literacy intervention. During the first month in class, Ma-Lee's silence was a felt presence: She rarely spoke, even in small groups, and when she did, in response to questions, I felt that it was only out of deference to authority. Any voluntary communication she made was whispered almost inaudibly to a classroom friend, Kari, who was also Hmong. There were several uncomfortable incidents during which visiting teachers mistook Ma-Lee's lack of participation as defiance and consequently reprimanded her. She would just lower her head, cover her mouth, and fall more deeply into herself, into her silence.

Ma-Lee's reluctance to speak did not signify submission or reticence; her silence was what the literary critic King-Kok Cheung (1993) might call an "articulate silence," a strategic means of assessing her surroundings so that her voice might eventually be heard. Or as Stephanie Carter (2001) has theorized, for many students of color, silence may not suggest the absence of meaning but instead be a form of critical discernment. On September 30, still early in the year, Ma-Lee put an essay on my desk. We had been having some class discussions about the idea of culture, and this was her response, in her own words:

> My family were in Thailand for 15 years. My mom and dad were
> embroiders in Thailand. I was born in Thailand. I didn't know
> about the Thai people, but my dad said Thai people were bad. We
> lived in the camp, but we had the U.N. serve food for my family.
>
> My parent were from Laos to Thailand. Their lives in Thailand
> were very hard because they had no money and [not] enough food
> for us.

> My family came here, because my country wast war. Vietnam took over so my parents can't stay there. My family immigrant in 1992.
>
> My family lives in U.S.A. It was very nice and so much different from my country,
>
> I feel about culture is difficult for me and maks me confused. I don't know what to be But think I want to be both cultures.

It became immediately obvious that Ma-Lee was a thoughtful child. Far from having a deficit, she reflected profoundly on her family's experiences and its implications for her present situation. Her autobiography became a means of gaining a critical distance from the past while making sense of the present. She wrote with the humble (and humbling) authority of a 10-year-old about a life that I, and probably many readers of this book, couldn't even begin to imagine. For me, the scale of hunger, malnutrition, disease, torture, and violence is necessarily abstract. For Ma-Lee and her family, there is no outside the border, no relatively autonomous safe space except, perhaps, her immediate home and community. The United Nations refugee camp becomes a synecdoche for her world. She is a foreigner wherever she goes; every place is a potential site of conflict and threat. Nevertheless, Ma-Lee invokes her past with judiciousness and clarity.

Ma-Lee's Autobiography: "My Culture Is the Right Way to Be"

The last few sentences of Ma-Lee's essay register a note of ambivalence about her most recent migration to Hmong America, a note that is not uncommon in much of my students' work. She is grateful for the ways in which the United States is nice, but at the same time feels confused about existing in both cultures. It appears that Ma-Lee's growth in my class involved organizing and transforming these confused and ambivalent sentiments into new, more empowering emotions and experiences. This process began with informal discussions. I invited Ma-Lee to join an open, flexible group of current and former students to talk about multiculturalism, or really any issues that were relevant to their lives.

Sometimes the group's meetings occurred during regular class time, but more often we met at lunch, during recess, and before or after school. In this "second classroom," Ma-Lee began to participate regularly. She spoke openly about her experiences in an ongoing dialogue that I believe had a profound impact on the other students. Together, they gained a deeper understanding of the particularity of one another's stories while at the same time coming to a more comprehensive view of their common vulnerabilities. Or rather, it was *through* shared insight into suffering and struggle that they could begin to hear and learn from one other and I from them.

Toward the end of the school year, Ma-Lee began to write something surreptitiously. She did this on her own time, during whatever we were supposed to be working on. I would pretend to sneak over to take a peek, and she would cover her paper or hide it in her desk. Eventually she handed in the following piece, titled "Autobiography of a Hmong Girl," fully typed and edited:

I was born in Thailand. My family was not rich. They worked hard just to make us grow and survive, but they were happy to stay how they were. We lived in Lao. My mom and dad were born in Laos. That time I was not born yet. One day Vietnamese came and took over Laos. My family migrated to Thailand because they had hoped there would be no more war and poverty. My family stayed there not long. Then I was born. I remember my cousin bought me candy. She also tried to take me to school with her, but she couldn't. It was forbidden to let anyone in school until they're 8 or 9 years old. That's why I didn't go to school.

We stayed in Thailand about three years. I had 4 brothers when we were still in Thailand. When my sister was born she died; she was supposed to be the biggest in our family. When I was 3 years old we immigrated to the United States. My dad tried to take me to school, but they said "you're too little to go to school." I was too small to go to kindergarten. So when I was five years old I went to school. I liked that school. It was the best school I ever went to. I had good friends. Their names were Ma-Lee, Jennifer, Ma-Lee, and Jennifer. My friend's names were like a pattern.

I stayed in school about five years because I started kindergarten and stayed until 4th grade. Then we moved here. When I first saw this school, I didn't like it. I said this school doesn't look like my old school. I liked my old school much better. When I came to this school everyone always made fun of us and always said we were Chinese people. So I felt bad about myself. I couldn't wait to go to fifth grade. When I came to fifth grade in Mr. Campano's class I think I was very fortunate. He always made people get better or feel better about themselves. So I think my culture is the right way to be.

No matter what people said about my culture, I pretended not to hear. Now it's May 4th, 2000. I'm going to sixth grade. I'll miss my teacher. We only have about four weeks to spend time and have fun together.

Now I will tell you a little bit about my people. In our Hmong culture we have to wake up very early to go to our garden. Even a little girl like me has to go. You also have to sew your own clothes. You can put red, blue, yellow or you can put any color you like. You can go to the store to buy it, but it costs a pack of money for just one dress, so we prefer to sew our Hmong clothes. We sewed clothes for ourselves, but we didn't even have shoes to wear.

I want everyone to know about my life and know how to respect my culture to make our Hmong people full of freedom. I know someday if no one wants to go out there and talk what they believe, I will because I don't want people to make fun of me and my culture. I know everyone wants to live in freedom. If someday my dreams come true, the world that I live in will always be radiant and never be dim with prejudice. This is what I believe in my heart.

Ma-Lee's story powerfully articulates her feelings and asserts her desire to be heard; her autobiography demonstrates the ways in which she organized "inchoate or confused feelings to produce an emotion that is experienced more directly and fully" (Mohanty, 1997, p. 206). This experience is both theoretical and political. Ma-Lee achieves a more focused and accurate understanding of the continued relevance and value of her culture as a source of insight that could guide action. She evaluates what has been meaningful to her, such as the friendships she cultivated in her old school as well as her family's former work embroidering, and her preference for making clothes and growing food in the garden. She also discusses the obstacles of coming to the United States, including the experience of having her ethnicity rendered invisible in the eyes of the majority culture. At the same time, Ma-Lee points toward a more universal need for everyone to live in freedom.

LEARNING TO LISTEN

It was striking to me how Priscilla's and Ma-Lee's survival stories were also ineluctably educational narratives. What I found most moving was that all these children, although from very different backgrounds, asserted their deep emotional investment in schooling. For them, schooling is much more than entitlement or status. Ma-Lee had been struggling to have access to education as long as she could remember. One salient pattern in her narrative was her repeated attempts to go to school with her cousin, despite her being too small. In a drawing Ma-Lee made of her family's refugee camp in Thailand, the temporary homes are part of the background,

Thailand Refugee camp

almost shading into the landscape in dull, grayish colors. What is in the foreground, in color and labeled, are the institutions: There is a United Nations tent; a sign pointing toward a hospital; and most prominently, a school.

Similarly, in her biography, Priscilla laments the lack of opportunities for Marilyn, who has to drop out of school and work, ironing and washing to support her family. The students project their future, their lives and livelihood, through education; unfortunately, schools often suppress the very histories that make learning matter, something worth uprooting and risking one's self for.

The children's growth in my class was at least partially predicated on our ability to create a classroom community that would encourage them to recognize the value of their own experiences. In addition, I needed access to a scholarly community that could help me interpret these very experiences. I would recruit colleagues to help me engage in "descriptive reviews" of the students' writing, a professional dialogue whose aim was "to recognize and specify a particular child's strength as a person, learner and thinker" (Carini, 2001, p. 4). The students' narratives, and my own process of reflecting on them, have enabled me to better "imagine," as Elaine Scarry (1996) might say, individual children in their full "weight and solidity" (p. 98). In the process, I became more mindful of their presence under teaching and learning conditions that could be described, in all fairness, as daunting and at times dehumanizing.

These imaginings ideally lead to alternative ways of structuring classroom space and time, different means of evaluation, new frameworks from which to recuperate the past to create meanings for the present and act to affect the future. Sometimes this type of work has a ripple effect outward into the school, maybe even the neighborhood, allowing the children's voices and their words to become more audible and empowering. The following year, in sixth grade, Ma-Lee's test scores rose substantially and she earned a medal in a highly rigorous academic pentathlon. Her story of achieving a more fully realized cultural identity was coextensive with her academic success.

But I think it's important to temper one's optimism. Although Ma-Lee, Priscilla, and other children were successful in my class, their educational futures remain uncertain because of systemic inequality. Only a small percentage of the neighborhood students eventually go on to higher education. I think, also, about the students who remain shrouded in the mystery of their own particular histories, students who have left my class as well as the new students to arrive in the fall. These are the ones who are silent or "defiant," the ones who are disciplined or just ignored because their value is unintelligible and foreign, whose mouths remain covered because we haven't learned how to listen. Until we can work more critically and imaginatively beyond our own insular institutional and cultural boundaries, it may be best to heed one of Ma-Lee's final observations: "There is more to a person's life than can fit on paper"—and, I would add, especially when the paper contains our own representations of a child's success, or failure.

CHAPTER 6

"They Came Here for Their Lives"

Writing Transnational Identities

To understand just one life, you have to swallow the world.
—Salman Rushdie, *Midnight's Children*

CONTRADICTING STEREOTYPES OF CHILDREN in segregated neighborhoods, my fifth graders did not write about merely narrowly provincial concerns. They did not lack background knowledge, and they were not disadvantaged, as a result of not having middle-class experiences, in their abilities to think abstractly or systematically, contrary to what some "specialists" on children in poverty would erroneously claim. Rather, their social locations afforded them the opportunity to think broadly and thoughtfully about serious intellectual and ethical issues in a cross-cultural framework. It is common for schools to say in their mission statements that they are preparing students to become productive global citizens. But many children are already productive global citizens.

In Chapter 4, I introduced Maria and discussed how she critiqued misrepresentations of her neighborhood. Maria, like many of my students, did not just develop a language of critique; she also used school literacy to interact with and shape the world, to act in it. Her literacy practices were procreative as well as critical. Following Lowe (1996), Maria's words were "immigrant acts" of "labor, resistance, memory and survival" that had real effects (p. 9). They were acts of agency that enabled her to reflect on a past history and chart a future, speculate about and inhabit the perspectives of others, and forge new relationships and responsibilities.

MARIA: WRITING FROM A *BALIKBAYAN* PERSPECTIVE

For Maria, writing became much more than an isolated school activity. It was part of a deeper inquiry into her emergent roles and responsibilities in both local and transnational contexts—a vehicle for defining her own evolving self-awareness as a Pinay from the south side of the city, as an American, *and* as a member of a greater diaspora. I sensed that her writing had a unique urgency and intimated possibility. It had urgency because she did not have the benefit of any obvious precedents: There are few works of literature or history for children that deal thoughtfully with Filipino/a Americans. It suggested possibility because, unencumbered by precedents, Maria was experimenting by drawing from a range of genres to name her experiences, as if she were discovering a new world, crafting original stories and, in the process, creating an audience for her work. This audience began in the classroom, then expanded outward to various neighborhood and public organizations.

A few weeks after she completed her response to the Cisneros vignette (see Chapter 4), Maria handed me the following additional paragraphs, which she felt were "very important":

> One more reason I believe the south side is in the heart is its spirituality. There are many people who are very spiritual. For example, many Filipino families that I know go to a teenager for support. They consider her as "the Healer." She has helped many people. The reason they go to her is because she has an aura of holiness. She is one of the chosen people, inhabited by the Holy Mother. What is so wonderful about her is that she is very open. She can help you, even if you don't know her. She already knows you. Another thing I believe is wonderful is that if you don't have much family, and if you don't attend church regularly, you can go to her. It is almost like a second home.
>
> I haven't been going to her house lately, but if I had the chance to go I would say, "thank you," because she has helped my family. She has helped my family endure sickness and loss. She has helped me a lot, and hopefully someday I can return to her with a gift.

The paragraphs describe an informal social and religious system that facilitates healing, reciprocity, and access to spiritual dimensions. The teenager is a "healer" who provides "a second home." One of the most important features of the "south side" is its "spirituality." Belying negative, danger-laden descriptions of urban life, the neighborhood is a space of safety, wonder, and rejuvenation.

Maria invites us to take her neighborhood seriously, to see it as a type of alternative space having an integrity and value of its own. In this and other of Maria's stories, and in her poems, I find a literary voice akin to that of magical realism (Zamora & Faris, 1995), a genre described as "suited to exploring—and transgressing—boundaries, whether the boundaries are ontological, political, geographical, or generic" (p. 5). In Maria's neighborhood we find the coexistence and comingling of different worlds, languages, and influences: a cultural hybridity. By investigating the particularity of her locale, I believe Maria paradoxically gained a cosmopolitan worldview and leverage against impoverished and impoverishing stereotypes and educational practices.

Maria was a voluminous writer. I have parsed the complexity of her output into three interwoven categories: school literacy as reflection, as an expression of empathy, and as correspondence. Maria employed school writing to reflect on her past in order to give meaning and purpose to her present and future. The losses she had endured and the dissonances in her life enabled her to speculate on the lives, perspectives, and vulnerabilities of others, whether those others were real or fictional, distant or familiar. This empathy not only infused her writing, but also contributed to the emotional tenor of our classroom. Finally, Maria wrote to correspond, reconstitute previous ties, and make new connections. Taken together, I hope my categories begin to convey the richness and sophistication with which children like Maria (re)create diaspora communities and transnational identities through literacy practices and as part of their daily lives in urban schools and neighborhoods.

"I'M GOING TO TALK TO YOU ABOUT MYSELF": SCHOOL LITERACY AS REFLECTION

Maria approached me for the first time when she was in fourth grade, to inform me that her mother had requested that I be her fifth-grade teacher. Maria wanted to let me know that she and her family were going through a difficult time, and she hoped that her studies would not be negatively affected. Her father had recently passed away, and she was still very sad. In addition, she would need to spend a lot of time with her younger sister, Tanya, while her mother worked.

It occurs to me in retrospect that Maria's introduction illustrated a coping strategy that was central to her social and educational development as well as to her writing. As I came to learn, she was open about the difficulties in her life, and she inserted herself into a set of supportive relationships. Similarly her story offered a means not only of working through, but also of making available or "objectifying," an interior state so that others might respond. She wrote to exteriorize what was once, as she wrote, "stored up in my heart and mind," so that it might be shared with those who cared. To *reflect*, in this sense, means not only "to thoughtfully consider," but also "to create a reflection, an artistic rendition or interpretation."

School literacy as an act of reflection provides children with the opportunity to (re)examine their lives and give form and meaning to their experiences. Maria's autobiography "My Life as a Pinay" frames her life as an ongoing response to a variety of challenges. It does not conform to the conventional immigrant narrative as a movement from poverty to refuge, often coded in nationalistic terms as a flight from third world turmoil to first world security. Rather, it is structured as a series of returns, both to the Philippines and to California. These returns are often occasioned by the death of loved ones, and the autobiography is thus a poignant meditation on loss as well. Loss and return are experiences from which Maria fashions an ethic of care and cooperation.

MY LIFE AS A PINAY

Have you ever had positive experiences in your life, a good or bad childhood, or even challenging experiences? Well, I've experienced all those things listed above, and I'm going to talk to you about myself in my autobiography.

I was brought into this world on February 14, 1990 in California. People say I'm so sweet and that I have a kind heart since I was born on Valentines Day. When I was about 8 months old I went to the Philippines for the first time in my life. I went there because my mom wanted to see my grandpa Leny's grave since he passed away four days before I was born; it could also mean that his spirit went into mine. We also went so that my family could see me for the first time and also because my grandma Isabel passed away. Even though I was a baby I still remember the scent of the sensational fruits and flowers. I didn't know my family yet, but soon to come I was going to know more and more as the years went by.

Unlike the traditional bildungsroman, which plots the (usually male) protagonist's maturation as a process of overcoming individual obstacles, Maria's autobiography describes her growth as the ongoing realization of her connectedness to others: "I didn't know my family yet, but soon to come I was going to know more and more." One of her earliest socially mediated recollections is of the coincidence of her grandfather's death with her own birth. The "spirit," for Maria both real and immaterial, functions as a means of asserting an intergenerational continuity that transverses vast geographical distances and transcends cultural dislocation. It is one way to both imagine and enact membership in a diaspora community. Maria's essay continues with the themes of birth and loss:

> On August 26, 1993 my little sister Tanya was brought into this world. I was three years old at that time. I was so naive at the time asking so many questions: "Daddy what's her name going to be?" "Mommy can I sleep with you and her?" They would just say, "Maria, you're our first baby." I liked it when they said that, but I was still envious of my sister. Although I had to bear in my mind that she was part of my family now and I loved her a lot.
>
> In June of 1994 my other grandpa died. It was my father's father. Everyone mourned his death. I shed such tears I couldn't stand to look at my grandfather's helpless and dead body. I didn't feel comfortable contemplating that my grandpa was not walking on earth, but I felt confident that he was walking with the guidance of our almighty God in a utopia. When it was the funeral, I thought in sorrow of the difficulties that my dad, aunts, uncles, cousins and everyone on my father's side would have. When it was time to let the undertakers (which were my family members) bury my grandpa I said my last few words: "Grandpa, sika ti Amang ko. Siyak ti apo kom. Ti ibagame kenyam Mahal Kita. Am-amen nga familiam." [You are my Grandpa. I am your grandchild. What we are going to tell you is that we love you. From all your family.] It felt very awkward the next few weeks. However we had to accept that grandpa Andre was dead. Three weeks after the burial, my father and I would have to leave the Philippines, but I would return that same year.

Through the recollection of the "scents of sensational fruits and flowers" and her use of the Ilocano language to recall her final words to her grandfather, the writing gives Maria's life in the Philippines an immediacy and strong presence. The autobiography goes on to describe subsequent trips to the Philippines in 1994 and 2000. In 1994, her "companions" were only her mother and sister. Her father stayed home because he did not want to "relive the pain" of returning home. Maria consequently felt guilt for "having fun." In her story Maria carefully reconstructs her heritage by naming her relative's specific towns. She then describes the differences between the Philippines and the United States; the joy of being with her cousins, who "raise her spirits"; and the naughty pleasure of learning how to drive at the age of 10. Then, toward the end of her last trip to the Philippines in February and March 2000, things "took an unexpected and sorrowful turn." Her father passes away. Time slows down, and the majority of the narrative is spent immersed in the events of mourning her father. The details become ever more precise. I quote this section at length:

On March 8, which was my Manaang Linda's birthday, my father passed away. The doctors in the Philippines say that my father was diagnosed with Leukemia. My family thought he died of heart problems. Well I guess he hid his Leukemia from my family because he wanted my sister and I to have a great vacation since I hadn't been there for six years. I can't believe he risked his life for three weeks.

A lot of people loved my father. When I called my family members, they began to cry. When they started to cry, I started to cry more. When they hung up I still heard them crying. I just couldn't believe my father was really gone, but when I found out the doctors didn't inject him yet I was a little happy. It was mandatory that doctors let the deceased person have a 24-hour waiting period. I prayed for a miracle. I went to see if my father's casket was gone, but it wasn't, so I knew he wasn't going to get the miracle I prayed for. I knew he was surely dead.

When my mom got home she told me that they were going to bring my dad at 12:00 noon. I stayed in my room doing nothing but crying until my dad was in the house. When they put his body on the stand, I noticed that people gave flowers from all over the world: Hong Kong, Hawaii, and the United States. A lot of people really loved and were close to my father. I thanked them for their gifts.

When people were done sitting by the casket, my mom told me to sit by my dad. It is something a person must do with deceased family members. People tried to cheer me up, but in my mind I said, "Why are you trying to cheer me up? My dad is gone now." At about 5:00 in the afternoon my father's family came. They of course brought their tears with them. The people who came were: Uncle Boy, Uncle Eddie, and my Uncle Lenny (my dad's twin); my auntie Bertha, my Uncle Paul's wife (I'm sorry I forgot your name Auntie), and my dad's cousins. Their names were Manang Kim, Manang Laura, Manong Albert, Manong Luke, and my Uncle Paul's son (Sorry, Manong that I forgot your name).

They came for one night, which was my dad's Last Night. Last Night means the night before burial. On the Last Night two people came who sang. Some of my family members sang as well. My Manang Kim sang "My Heart Will Go On" by Celine Dion. After she was finished, she said this, "Uncle, you will stay with us forever." I wanted to say something also, but I didn't feel like it. It was just stored in my heart and mind. Also on Last Night people come and gamble. The whole thing went on throughout the night. I stayed up. It was the last night that I would sleep with my father on earth.

In the morning I had to take a shower since it was the day of my Father's funeral. The funeral would start at 9:00, but it was transferred to 9:30 because the church had just finished their mass. When I went back to my house I still had time to change. My clothing had to be black. That is one other thing that the people in town do when someone is dead in their family. When it was time to let the people take my father's body to the car I started to cry. I knew that in less than 1 hour my father would not be seen on Earth. When I walked outside I couldn't believe what was before my eyes. A lot of people came to attend my father's funeral. Everyone was crying. I knew in my heart that people really enjoyed my dad.

Then when we got to the Church my cousins carried my dad's casket. I stopped crying when I sat down in the seat. In the funeral there was singing, and giving praise to my father and the family.

At the end of the funeral people put flowers on my father's mirror. It was time again to let the family members take my dad's casket and put it into the car. When we started walking I didn't cry. We took the longer way to the cemetery. My father would be buried by my Auntie Maria (which is who my cousin and I are named after) and my Grandpa's grave.

When we got to the place where my father would be buried I looked at my father for the last time. I knew that this was the moment to speak my heart to show him how much I loved him. I said, "Daddy, I know you are going to be with the Lord. Say hello to everyone in Heaven. Remember we will love and keep you in our hearts forever. I know that when I die I won't be afraid because all of you will be waiting for me or anyone else in the sky." Those were my last words from my mouth to my father. I knew he was looking down on my family from Heaven. When my father was still alive he told me to reach my goal. I told him I would reach my goal. I would put my heart to it and make him proud of me.

Maria used autobiography to gain a certain distance from the past while retaining its relevance for the present. One way she coped with her father's death was by describing in detail the mourning ritual of Last Night, suffusing it with emotional and spiritual significance. Her description of loss shifts between expressions of an internal, inarticulate state, "I couldn't say anything," to vivid and meticulous perceptions of a surrounding world of vitality and communion. Maria is not simply confined within the closed circuit of suffering; bereavement is portrayed as a social and cultural process that insists on meaning and dialogue. Her words rise to heaven, but they also reach laterally to those living kin who are at once strange and familiar, or in her words, to "whom I know and do not know." This linked her to a community that stretches from Hong Kong to Hawaii and California:

> My life right now as a bicultural Pinay is very exciting. Being bicultural, or *balikbayan*, is fun because we have a lot of traditions and dances. For example, I saw the Tinikling dance at the town fiesta 2000. One of the other great advantages of being Filipino is that Filipinos are very religious. Some cities go to church three or four days a week. It is also a good place to catch a glimpse of a ghost. I have seen about six ghosts in my life. Five of them were part of my family. The other was the "White Lady," as we tend to call her. She's very pretty. She was like an angel from Heaven, her hair so long and soft like a pillow, and her kind smile like a baby sighing. I wanted to do something such as say, "*Kumasta*," but she vanished as fast as the wind. I will never forget those wonderful moments, even though I was supposed to be frightened.

Maria's relationship to her past experiences in the Philippines may be considered a type of "reflective nostalgia." According to Svetlana Boym (2001), this sense of longing "opens up a multitude of potentialities" and "has a capacity to awaken multiple planes of consciousness" (pp. 49–50). It invites narratives that reveal how "longing and critical thinking are not opposed to one another, as affective memories do not absolve one from compassion, judgment or critical reflection" (pp. 49–50). In Boym's typology, it is contrasted with "restorative nostalgia," which attempts a return to an ideal time or location, a perfect state frozen in history. We hear the accents of restorative nostalgia when teachers lament a halcyon past when children knew more, when parents were supportive and the neighborhood safe, when there were fewer "foreigners." I found that many of my students and their families were reluctant to overly romanticize any one time, place, or way of life. Maria's autobiography decries the wars in the Philippines, saying, "I can't believe my people would do such a thing, to each other, to anybody"; but for another assignment she has also written indignantly about being "invisible twice" in the United States, as a Filipina, a female, and a member of an ethnic minority. Or, even more disturbingly, she has described being hypervisible when she was the target of racial epithets by passing strangers.

I believe that the experiences of many immigrant students—of being outsiders and living in between cultures—alert them to ambiguity, complexity, and the possibilities for loss and conflict. Through storytelling, students may reflect on their more dissonant experiences and in the process cultivate a sense of empathy, balance, and critical judgment. Nostalgia may serve the present by being the muse for the future. Maria used to say, alluding to Carlos Bulosan, that her "words go from the heart to the world and back again." In her autobiography, Maria re-collects the past and organizes her experiences to generate new meanings. Her goal of becoming a doctor is not just a professional ambition; it is an opportunity to ameliorate the bodily pain of others and provide medicine for poorer relatives. The loss of family members is not just loss; it creates a time to become closer with family. Maria's mobility is not only disorientating; it becomes a guiding intellectual and imaginative force that enables her to at once value individuality and our commonalties, her own ethnic *roots* and *routes* of intercultural understanding. Maria transforms the problem of belonging into the virtue of multiple belongings and the longing for a more tolerant world. She concludes:

> Now if you're bicultural, or a mixture you should be proud of it and say you're a unique person. Don't internalize negativity. You're you!! That is just one of my mottoes. Mottoes are sayings that have special meanings. I think we are all wonderful and should tolerate one another. My life has been like a roller coaster. It is filled with great moments and depressing moments, but no matter what happens, I say I'm proud to be *balikbayan*, I'm proud to be Pinay.

This is her protean cultural lens that shapes her locale and the consciousness of our classroom. Its value cannot be measured by standardized-test scores or writing rubrics. It is not amenable to five-paragraph essays.

"THIS WAS A DAY THAT HAD SWOLLEN MY HEART": SCHOOL LITERACY AS EMPATHY

Over time the boundaries of our class became porous, open to the voices, sentiments, and hopes of people in the neighborhood and loved ones abroad. A symbiotic relationship developed; the students adapted school literacy to reflect on their places in the world, and I in turn became more concerned with this larger world and adjusted the curriculum accordingly. The pressures to run efficiently through standardized curricula were balanced by the desires to address and be addressed by individual children and their families. This involved a shift in how I thought about the goals of schooling. Instead of just measuring the degrees to which students were adapting to school, I also concerned myself with how school can be transformed from within by the knowledge and experiences of the students themselves.

Schools are traditionally competitive and individualistic. Students are often required to distinguish themselves from others, and in the process they sometimes begin to understand themselves as inferior. This is perhaps one context within which we can see the significance of Maria's phrase "Don't internalize negativity." Empathy is a counterpoint to such internalization; its reach is outward, sometimes extending across time and space. It is characterized by an initial capacity to differentiate between self and other (so as to not overidentify) in order to vicariously imagine, feel compassion for, and express solidarity with another's condition. In this process, the self may be transformed as well. Maria's writings repeatedly display empathetic sensibilities. In her autobiography, she is mindful of the "sorrow and tears" of those who have come to share her grief.

In another of her essays, "My Memorable Holiday Thought," Maria elaborates on the emotions she feels for family and friends in the Philippines:

> When we got to my home, my mother's home, my heart radiated with such delight that I could feel it elevate to where I shed tears like a water fountain. I could surely see this was a day that had swollen my heart. When I finally could start to talk I said, "Manangs, Manongs, Uncles, Aunties, all of us are once again reunited. Let's make this trip of mine the most memorable. With Guidance of our Lord, Amen." We all couldn't overcome the astonishment of seeing each other over what seemed a myriad of endless years. I felt like we were segregated in the world. I felt indignant that my family and I were put in this harsh and unfair situation. My birthday was not part of our conversation until a few hours later. They expressed how much had changed without the "Balikbayans'" presence. "Maria, you're back! I missed you so much!" my cousin hailed. When she got down from the balcony, she embraced me as tight as you would hug a family member you haven't seen for decades. I felt very contented, even though I could hardly breathe. After we had finished embracing, she looked at me and started to sob tears. "Manang," I said, "You and I will always be cousins. You can always talk to me and I will try to understand your situation," I said in a way to make her feel my heart and soul. We spoke for an abundance of hours in the wonderful colorful pastures while eating fruits with pleasurable delight. We wagged

our tongues about people we thought had wonderful etiquette. We also gossiped about those we found kind of rude. Then we talked about our studies.

In this essay Maria describes the sensations provoked by mutual care and recognition and expresses her desire to understand another's situation. The love of a relative becomes physically transferred to her body: her heart "radiated"; she felt it "elevate" as it became "swollen" with emotion. Maria's writing has an epistolary quality. It is composed with an intimate audience in mind, and her words are a prism that refracts the intentions and emotions of a potential respondent. In our classroom Maria's concern for others was contagious. It translated in turn into our concern for her, her family, and the issues that have shaped and continue to shape her life. Soon all the children began to write about their friends in other towns, states, and countries.

We eventually commemorated our global ties on a bulletin board whose heading was "Nurturing the Diaspora: To Our Friends and Family Abroad." We hung photos of our *manangs, manongs, tias,* and *tios,* our aunties, uncles, and cousins. We displayed letters and essays from or about our relatives. It was an opportunity to transform family history into a collective inquiry into our shared space, an opportunity to turn the accidents of history into the intentions of community. The children kept tabs on one another. They asked about one another's families and homes. The students became familiar with one another's migrant stories, with the play of choice that formed the enriching diversity of our classroom, school, and neighborhood. The students also used the bulletin board as a lens out onto the world. For example, they decided to do research about topics such as world poverty, focusing on the shanties of Manila's poorest neighborhoods; child slavery; and the human-trafficking industry. Many of the students were able to draw on the experiences of people they knew in order to discuss these topics.

As we became acquainted with one another's family groups, an idiom of kinship developed in our class. I observed my students engaging in acts of empathetic displacement that drew attention away from the self to the other. This dynamic may have been especially important for those children who had become dislocated and were living in what Maria described as "a segregated world." An awareness of the precariousness of community imparted the wisdom that it must not be taken for granted; it must be imagined, worked for, created, and re-created. For example, Maria and a number of the other students started what we called a buddy project. They decided to "adopt" children in some of the younger grades. They wrote

them encouraging letters and tutored them with their homework. Empathetic transactions were a means of preserving old social relations and creating new ones. They were also pedagogical opportunities. More than mere sentiment, empathy allowed children to cultivate critical and ethical sensibilities in order to understand and inhabit the perspectives of others.

One of Maria's final texts for my class was a novella titled "The War That Changed Lives and Altered Perspectives." She described the piece as falling into the genre of historical fiction, inspired by stories passed down to her by her grandfather. She translated oral history into a classroom assignment about an episode in American history that has been elided in most textbooks, the aftermath of the Philippine-American war. This is how Maria's novella begins:

Around the year 1922 a family emigrated from the Philippines. No big deal, right? Wrong. They didn't come here by choice; they came here for their lives. Their lives were at serious risk because the American military threatened their whole community in Illocos Norte. The community contained 1,800 people. Fortunately some families fled the land and the country. But some were treated like slaves and were prosecuted [persecuted]. However, their souls were going to look down from the celestial clouds on the people who were trying to escape the land.

Maria's story is too long to quote in its entirety—it runs about 15 single-spaced typed pages. It centers on the endangered lives of a Filipino family as they try to escape the oppression of a sadistic American military commander. Maria orchestrates a polyphony of voices in a rich text that draws from multiple discursive resources. It incorporates, in addition to her family's oral tradition, Filipino, epistolary, idiomatic dialogue and more formal school prose influenced by novels Maria had been reading. Through writing, she imaginatively occupied the "perspectives" of a diverse range of multifaceted characters. For example, she describes John Ray, an "unorganized," "tumultuous," and "idle" student whose clandestine love of reading and writing become a means of personal transformation:

> He didn't pay much attention to school. They thought he wouldn't get into college. What his friends and family didn't know is that he loved to read and write. They were his virtues. He wouldn't take it serious at school, but he took it serious at home. One of his favorite books was by Jose Rizal. It changed his life. It was about freedom: "Writing comes from the heart and soul, and your heart and soul should be put on paper," John Ray would say to himself. He was just too timid to tell people of his other side.

Maria also wrote about an American soldier, Carl, who had to negotiate the dilemma of executing orders or helping to free innocent Filipino captives. She injected into this potentially one-dimensional figure a moral consciousness:

> When Carl opened the cabinet, he took out the files of the captives. While Carl was browsing through the files he stopped to think to himself, *How come most of the people who are held captive are poor and innocent? How come they chose the weak? Wait a minute, what am I realizing? I want to help the Filipinos, not persecute them. I should just*

stop thinking for now and get all these files into a bag. If I get caught there will be no chance for me to help.

Carl defies orders and eventually helps a Filipino family escape. Ironically, the family escapes to their "new home" in America.

Although not autobiographical, Maria's text may be considered a narrative of decolonization in that it displays critical awareness of the historical factors that have helped create contemporary Filipino America: colonization, poverty, displacement, and the desire to find and redefine a safe home.

"PART OF MY LIFE WAS REFILLED INTO MY MIND": SCHOOL LITERACY AS CORRESPONDENCE

My contribution to our bulletin board in honor of friends and family abroad were letters from distant relatives in the Philippines. They were often written in both English and Visayan, and Celso, Maria, and other children would help translate. The students themselves started to bring in letters and pictures from abroad. We would speculate about cross-family patterns in this type of transnational literacy practice. The airmail envelopes, bordered with red, white, and blue bands, were often stamped with portraits of Jose Rizal, artifacts intimating membership in a large global citizenship. The materiality of the letters themselves called attention to their worldliness, to the material location from which they were produced. Many were often typed on thin paper, smudged by ink and whiteout.

One student observed that the letters were bilingual. Formal greetings were written in English and then the letters would transition into Filipino languages to invoke a sense of family obligation. We noted that the letters made references to how difficult life could be in the more impoverished regions of the Philippines. In one of my own letters, a relative wrote of how "the rich become richer, the poor become poorer"; how there is no "economic, political or social stability"; and how my relative's "sons and daughters struggle hard just to eat and live." Another requested assistance to pay for a basic medical procedure. What follows is a portion of one uncle's letter that conveys both familiarity and distance:

Mis. Or.
July 27, 1998
Dearest Nephew,
    Peace, Love, Joy . . .
    Greetings from Misamis Oriental, Phils.!

I received your letter and am very happy, that you take concern for the family here, the life of your grandfather in the Philippines.

Well, I have nothing to say so much, I'll just relate to you something.

Only your grandfather is still alive and can still share to you the testimonies of his life.

As far as I know, your grandfather is a handsome man in his young days, the townsfolk were impressed the way he played guitar. Your grandfather has many sweethearts.

Your grandfather was born in a small village which was part of Talisayan. It is a beautiful place with a small wharf facing the Pacific ocean. The people are peace-loving and pure Catholic. Fishing, farming and some handicraft are the only source of livelihood. But now the village is progressive with sea and land transportation.

If you want to visit the Philippines, just inform us in advance when you plan to visit here so we can fetch you from the airport.

Good night and sweet dreams across the miles. We are looking forward to your forthcoming visit here in the Philippines.

We love and miss you so much.

Loving Uncle

The emotion found in this tenuous correspondence from one country to the other may be all the more effusive because it has to communicate across geographical, generational, and cultural boundaries. I do not know my relatives in the Philippines. The correspondences aspire to reconstruct endangered memory and buried history.

Taken together, the letters reveal that longing—a desire to both know where one has come from and where others have gone—goes both ways across the Pacific. Although its component parts are inspired by different circumstances and motivated by different needs, this mutuality, this cor-respondence of longing, represent the conditions within which to re-create transnational bonds. This form of literacy practice refers not only to literal correspondence—that is, letters, phone calls, or e-mails—but also to an underlying commitment to establish a common interest. Literacy as correspondence generates meaning through the perceiving of relationships and the discovery of commonalities across oceans of difference. This ex-panding web of communication and care may be related to the Tagalog word *tayo*—the word, as Leny Mendoza Strobel (2000) has reminded the academic community, that means an inclusive "we," an indigenous Fili-pino value that sees no "inside/outside" duality (p. 366).

This type of correspondence raises questions about the role of teachers in diverse classrooms. We too are limited by our own experiences; at the same time, we find ourselves compelled to teach sensitively and thoughtfully across a wide range of boundaries. Our relationships with our students may not always feel natural or automatic. It is doubtful that we can ever acquire sufficient knowledge of all their backgrounds to facilitate easy identifications, much less transparent intercultural communication.

How can we begin to create correspondence, community, within the diversity of our school and neighborhood? What are our obligations to one another? On what foundation are the obligations based? Can we forge a solidarity that takes difference as an asset rather than as a problem or deficit? As a teacher researcher, I found that these became my ongoing inquiries. The narratives of children such as Maria, who exist at the nexus of longings, help me begin to fill in these gaps:

> All those wonderful moments wouldn't just stay there in the Philippines, they would linger in my heart. When it was our turn to give our plane tickets for the States, they also took our boxes. It took a long time because there were seven of us. It would have been eight, but my father passed away. After they checked everything, we went to sit down. As the minutes came closer for our flight, I said my prayer, "Lord . . . please give my family here guidance. If their lives go well, then there is no one to thank but you. Tell my father he is welcome to join us and you, since he doesn't need a ticket. With your love and blessing, Amen."
>
> When we were in the air, I was feeling good because now I knew what the Philippines was like. I felt a little better because part of my life was refilled into my mind once again. I was kind of elated and melancholic at the same time. After about thirty minutes, they started distributing food to people. As I was eating my food, I looked out the window to find myself over the vast ocean. I started to contemplate what it feels like being a member of the Filipino diaspora.
>
> Filipinos are dispersed all throughout America, Canada, and the world. The usual thing that happens is that they become accustomed to their new lives and make friends, and they feel content that they have better lives. But there are also negativities that might happen if they experience racism, miss home, join gangs, or have problems putting a roof over their heads. We can all make mistakes, but I will try not to because of love and support from my family and all the neighbors in my area. When I grow up,

I'll become a doctor and travel around the world to take care of those who are poor. In the future, one of my dreams is that we will have a tolerant world without violence or prejudice, where everyone is a pacifist, even though I know the only utopia is in heaven.

REACHING BEYOND THE SCHOOL CURRICULUM

By inviting me into their neighborhood, students such as Maria challenged me to explore resources beyond the school curriculum. These resources include family stories as well as interpretive frameworks drawn from disciplines such as ethnic and minority studies. The students, in turn, directly and indirectly used these resources to help create more empowering cosmopolitan identities for themselves. The students' examinations of their ethnicity and my effort to respond to the diversity of my class became inseparable contexts of inquiry. In these types of cooperative processes, students make possible new understandings of a world that remains largely invisible to those outside "the neighborhood."

In fact, however, the isolated ethnic neighborhood, or enclave, and its attendant stereotypes no longer provide a useful model for understanding the lives and learning of immigrant children. As anthropologists have pointed out, the local is formed by outside forces. Maria's neighborhood may be better understood as an archipelago, like the Philippines: each residence an island, a diverse environment unto itself, the streets routes of cultural exchange and flow, linked to greater political, economic, and social dynamics. The students were connected to a number of different geographical locations. As a consequence, their work was often animated by affective, intellectual, and cultural affiliations that exceeded political borders, neighborhood boundaries, and restrictive social categories.

I believe that the status of immigrant alone implies a degree of informed, self-respectful agency: the ability to interpret personal and familial conditions and move toward greater freedom. Maria built on her immigrant legacy by populating her locale with memories, languages, artifacts, spirits, and expressive practices, creating a protean cultural lens through which to analyze and potentially transform the realities of her life. Maria's writings went against dominant paradigms of school writing as a mimetic representation of a generic institutional model, for example, using the protocols of a commercial literacy program that requires students to produce five-paragraph essays in a 45-minute period, which teachers evaluate by using a rubric. I have found that these types of writing assignments often become separated from their creators, usually serving only bureaucratic interests. Maria's words, by contrast, were very much of her world and, following Freire, by being of it, partook in its constitution. The *world* in this context can be understood somewhat literally. Maria's actual, intellectual, and emotional neighborhood is an example of the local swallowing the global, compelling educators to expand our own provincial notions of what counts as knowledge and curriculum.

CHAPTER 7

Dancing Across Borders

Performing Identities

So if they say anything, say why is it?
—"No Rest for the Weary," Blue Scholars, hip-hop duo

D URING MY LAST TWO YEARS as a fifth-grade teacher researcher I had the fortune of collaborating with Angelica, a student teacher in the California Mini-Corps program. Mini-Corps's mission is to mentor undergraduate college students who intend to teach in schools with high concentrations of migrant students, and who are themselves from migrant backgrounds. In addition to majoring in education, Angelica was completing a minor in the performance arts. She had great passion for her artistic talents in drama, dance, and puppetry, and I encouraged her to incorporate her talents in her teaching.

One day Angelica was criticized by a usually supportive administrator for engaging students with drama. They were improvising a piece that incorporated theatrical movements with the children's own spoken-word poetry and writings from Francisco Jimenez, Maya Angelou, and Carlos Bulosan, authors who all had personal or activist ties to the neighborhood and surrounding areas. Angelica's competence was not in question. Her talents as both an educator and an artist were well respected in the community and showcased at our school's annual multicultural festival. What was at issue was the time. It was 9:15 a.m., somewhere in the middle of the school's literacy block. Apparently an artistic/literacy practice that involved reading, writing, listening, speaking, cooperating, using local literary traditions, interpreting texts through body language, and drawing on rich life experiences did not count as official literacy. In a school subject to instructional mandates that emphasized the transmission of skills through codified programs, the administrator was, perhaps reasonably, unsettled: "What if my boss visits the school and all the students are not on the same page?" she queried.

THE PERSONAL AS PROFESSIONAL

From the very first moment we begin teaching, we bring our life histories to bear upon our practice. Our presence in the classroom is ineluctably animated by our own experiences as learners, our implicit and explicit notions of what constitutes knowledge, and what it means to be an educated person. These shape the contours of what we imagine as being possible in the classroom. They also expose our vulnerabilities. As it is with students, so it is with teachers.

When our personal trajectories lead us within the contexts of schooling, we engage in subtle, and often not fully conscious, assimilations and negotiations. Professional discourses and practices may regulate what aspects of one's history will be denied or compromised, and what aspects may be brought to the fore. These denials and compromises may be especially salient for new teachers who themselves were, or continue to be, "nontraditional" students, teachers whose own cultural and class-based experiences may fit uneasily with the norms of education. One of the ongoing inquiries presented in this book is how these norms may circumscribe, but ultimately not define, teaching and learning in an ethnically diverse public elementary school. New teachers may be constrained by personal history, especially when they are evaluated by social criteria that has very little to do with their potential. However, this history may also be an educator's greatest asset, imbuing teaching with passion and giving it intellectual focus.

There is a pervasive trend in current teaching organizations as well departments of education to establish a consensus on the best ways to teach in order to bring about uniformity across schools and sometimes districts. In professional development workshops and training sessions, the term *research based* is often invoked to appeal to and establish the authority of best practices that "work." Once teachers have access to these best practices, students will learn. Yet what works is itself a contested category, informed by some of our most deeply held values. Is working only measured by annual gains in test scores? Or does it also have to do with eventual access to higher education? Is unsettling one's determined social trajectory by thinking critically about one's life and choices an example of working? Can we ever know with certainty that our pedagogy has worked for the communities in which we teach?

How we imagine educational success is neither neutral nor unmediated by theoretical beliefs, assumptions, and social or cultural identities. Teachers are thus put in contradictory situations. They are prodded, and sometimes coerced, to adopt uniform curricula that may ultimately amount to their deskilling. At the same time, if teachers were to be automatons, uncritically executing programs and methods, they would likely meet resistance from both the administration and the students. Teachers are meant to stand out as individuals, to radiate a special social persona and demonstrate the ability to effectively adjust to and teach all children. Certain teachers are held up as exemplars for the rest to follow.

Teachers' roles are thus caught between pressures to conform to strictures of outside authorities and an expectation that they assert their own uniqueness in the classroom to facilitate student learning. For many, this may not be a real choice. Both roles, of conformist and of the exemplary individual, presuppose a hierarchical concept of knowledge. In the first case, knowledge is elsewhere, generated by specialists and researchers and transmitted down to teachers. In the second, knowledge becomes some essential and mysterious individual trait, often left unexamined. Sometimes it is considered tacit or unconscious knowledge, acquired through practice. Other times it is an extension of one's personality—some people are born to teach; they are naturals.

What is lost in this binary is any deep understanding of the ways that teachers themselves may respond to this predicament and make sense of teaching and learning, especially in neighborhoods characterized by poverty and segregation. The professional knowledge of teaching is not a static, abstract body of information. Rather, it is an ongoing act of creation that occurs when teachers adopt a critical inquiry stance in their classrooms. For Angelica, as we shall see, this knowledge was partially embodied, communicated through the motions of performance art. She spent her life figuratively and literally dancing across borders. Dancing becomes an apt metaphor to describe the "knowledge-of-practice" (Cochran-Smith & Lytle, 1999) in ethnically diverse settings, where knowledge is not fixed but is an everyday, living process of investigation, improvisation, and action.

"THE WORLD OUTSIDE OUR DOOR WAS FOREIGN"

Angelica credited her Mini-Corps advisor for being the first to recognize her capacities and to teach her how to work. By *work* she meant becoming a creator by having the position and resources to actively shape the dynamics of her community. In her time with Mini-Corps, Angelica has taught hundreds of children and staged performances in venues ranging from a neighborhood Cinco de Mayo festival, a talent night at a local community college, a school function called Multicultural Day in a neighborhood park, academic conferences, and a class on Chicano literature and cultural studies at Stanford University. Angelica achieved greater objectivity about the experiences, potential, and needs of migrant students by teaching *as* a migrant, letting her own identity as a migrant infuse her pedagogy. Teaching as a migrant involves self-conscious acts of remembrance, of keeping the past relevant, however difficult this may be. It involves an acknowledgment that the migration is not over, that the trails toward personal and collective empowerment are still being blazed.

In the process of interviewing the families of Spanish-speaking children, Angelica reflected on those teachers in her own life who maintained high expectations for her by providing the requisite intellectual and emotional support to attend college. At the same time, when children were admonished for speaking Spanish, she recalled how her first language became a marker of academic deficiency and defiance. When a parent laments that a teacher misunderstood her son, Angelica understands. In middle school, Angelica herself was publicly derided and sent home because of her inability to articulate, in English, a conflict at recess. When a child has difficulty getting to school on time because of familial obligations, such as the daily ritual of getting younger siblings ready, Angelica related how taxing it can be just trying to accomplish the tasks required to increase one's opportunities; for example, how she used to spend 3 hours a day on public buses traveling back and forth to and from a local college that was only several miles from her home.

But it was Angelica's direct experience with loss—with abrupt geographical, cultural, and emotional dislocation—that has provided her with special insight into the lives of so many of our students. When she was a young child, her mother migrated to California from her small town in Mexico in search of a sustainable life for her children. Angelica initially stayed behind, with her grandparents. In seventh grade, she joined her mother, first in Los Angeles and then to settle more permanently in our city. The transition was so painful that for a whole year after her departure from Mexico she was unable to talk to her grandparents over the phone; her words became too choked with tears. She longed for the freedom of her family's ranchero in Mexico:

> When I got to the States the most striking difference was that I did not have the freedom to roam, to climb trees, visit neighbors, and play with the animals. This is important for a child, I think. There

was this sense that I had to stay by the house, that there was something dangerous, unsafe, out there, that the world outside our door was foreign. The world was closing in on me.

Angelica's movements became geographically and socially circumscribed. She felt that her world was closing in, impinging on her former sense of movement and access. Under these circumstances, the performance arts—acting, the spoken word, puppetry, but especially dance and *teatro*—became a tonic for her distress and isolation. "I finally began to adapt to the States," she said "when I became more involved with dance, first in high school, and then in college." That art form took on an important existential role. Angelica felt most free when practicing, either in collaboration with a group or in the solitude of her room. Through participation in the performance arts, she could fully express herself and retain a sense of psychic autonomy and freedom. Like the members of the Latina Feminist Group who wrote their book *Telling to Live* (2001) to inspire young Latinas, Angelica yearned for "creativity" and employed the medium of dance to restore a "sense of wholeness" (p. 8).

Angelica's exploration of her own life story, her *testimonio*, informed her ongoing development as an educator. The Latina Feminist Group (2001) defines *testimonio* as a "form of expression that comes out of intense repression or struggle" that may serve both a personal and a political function. For Angelica, *testimonio* also served a professional function. Arriving at a deeper critical consciousness about her own identity was inseparable from how she thought about the purposes of teaching. In an educational climate that initiates young teachers into the profession by teaching standardized practices, *testimonio* may be considered an act of resistance.

LESSON PLANS: GIRL TALK AND *TEATRO*

The students' use of *teatro* was not merely the result of an activity or set of strategies that Angelica implemented in the classroom. Rather, it was an organic outgrowth of the relationships she had cultivated with the students over time. Angelica had, in fact, begun as an observer. Most days, after school or during break, we would debrief. Our conversations were more often about the children's social and emotional adjustments than about any specific teaching strategy. An awareness of the children as complete human beings preceded academic designations or instructions.

As Angelica acclimated herself to the classroom learning environment, she would unobtrusively engage students by helping them with their tasks or inquiries. Perhaps her most powerful pedagogical move was to share with the students her own life as a migrant—her *testimonio*. The students, in turn, began to open up to her, especially several of the girls whose primary language was Spanish. They drew pictures for her and wrote her letters and notes.

Angelica wanted to address these children's thoughts, concerns, and emotions so she organized a "Girl Talk" learning group (see Waff, 1994). She and her students read stories and poems together. Eventually they started multilingual reader-response journals, with prompts arising out of their conversations and readings. Angelica wrote back to the students weekly, and they wrote to one another. It was seemingly important for the students to feel as if they could write in evaluation-free zones. In this nurturing environment, the children's school literacy began to show considerable progress. According to Angelica, several of the children who had been reticent to participate began to initiate discussions and orally elaborate ideas. Others developed an avocation for journaling and letter writing. They soon studied dance, puppetry, and drama and formed a performance art group called Dancing Across Borders, which included a number of the boys in the class as well. Angelica related to me that one of her goals was to communicate to the students an expansive sense of who they could become; she was concerned that society imparted restricted roles for students, especially for girls, from minority communities.

One of Angelica's advisors once asked her if she had yet learned to make lesson plans in our class. She meant the kind of lesson plans that could be taught to any students in any classroom. Angelica and I decided that she had developed lessons that involved substantial planning around the students' experiences and interests, as well as her own ever-evolving stance as an educator. They were learning experiences being built from the ground up.

The cultural productions of Dancing Across Borders drew on the local tradition and history of El Teatro Campesino, a troupe that performed Chicano/a political theater and that arose from the migrant labor camps in the 1960s and 1970s. Yolanda Broyles-González (1994) states that the artistic practices of the acting ensemble were inseparable from the life practices of its members; "performance was viewed as part of the material social processes" of life and "always entailed consciousness of community and one's sense of belonging in the life of the community" (p. 87). In keeping with the spirit of the original El Teatro Campesino, the scripts were "living texts," written collaboratively and often altered in the context of practice and performance. Thus the process of composing the dramas pushed against the prevailing school ideology of individual authorship. There was no one author. It was genuinely a cooperative project. The work also resonated with conceptualizations of how drama can be a vehicle for students to imaginatively inhabit the perspectives and experiences of others in order to help craft critical and ethical perspectives (see Edmiston, 2000; Wolf & Enciso, 1994; Medina, 2004).

"¡CUANDO TODOS SOMOS IGUALES!" (WHEN WE ARE ALL EQUAL!)

The students' first work was a skit about the interwoven histories of Mexican and Filipino farmworkers in California's Central Valley. It was originally performed in three languages at a back-to-school night and involved the participation of parents and grandparents. The skit was introduced by several students who shared personal vignettes:

JASMINE (moderator): We are our parents' and grandparents' dreams. We are making our worlds in the present, and we are the future. We are proud to be multicultural. We are proud to live in a city that has inspired many important people: Maxine Hong Kingston, Maya Angelou, Dolores Huerta, and Carlos Bulosan. We read their stories, but there are many other stories and memories to be told.

KP: My name is KP. I am Pinoy. When my parents came to this country, they worked in the fields. The work was grueling and the wages were low. We also grew plants and fruit in the backyard to survive. Now my parents are Aleskeros. Twice a year they migrate to Alaska to work on fishing boats and in canneries. It is exhausting work, but they are happy to provide for their family. My dream is to get an education to give back to them someday.

LUIS: My name is Luis. I am Mexipino. My great-grandparents emigrated from the Philippines. My grandparents came from Mexico to escape poverty. They all worked in the fields. They also worked very hard to provide for their families. I like having numerous cultures to choose from. My dream is to be in the navy, like my dad, and retire comfortably.

MA-LEE: My name is Ma-Lee. My parents immigrated to Hmong America from Thailand. They came here because of war and poverty. We are happy to be here, to have opportunities. My dream is to have my education and make money for my family.

JASMINE: We are not separate but together. Our histories weave together like an intricate tapestry. In order to visualize a future without prejudice and suffering, we must first appreciate the past. This play is entitled "Dancing Across Borders!" It's about our ancestors, how they came together to declare their rights. We hope you enjoy it!

The play then opens with a grandfather reminiscing to his grandchildren about his migration to California: "I sailed here to California in the year 1929. I was told money grows from trees in California. I landed in San Francisco and moved to our city. That's where the story begins." The following scene portrays two recent migrants signing up for seasonal work at an agricultural company. Soon they are bent over in the fields, taking breaks only to read letters from their respective homelands that lend purpose to their labor:

Dearest Wilfred,
Life over here is very hard. We made 10 pesos selling chicken eggs in five hours, but we are happy to be alive. How are you doing? We are doing fine but Terry got hurt by the one-mile race. He hasn't fully recovered yet. Hope you still remember how good is our one-mile race festival. This year they had some games, delicious *adobo*, and big and new horses in the race. Please be safe.
Always,
Rodel

Compadre Fernando,
Gracias por prestarme los 25 pesos que le pedí, ya mis gallinas se morían de hambre. Compadre, que Dios se los pague, ¿porque pues yo quién sabe cuando? A lo mejor cuando me den mi aguinaldo. Todos lo extrañamos muchísimo compadre, con decirle que hasta sus vacas se pusieron flacas cuando se fue. Con la única novedad compadre que ya nació el hijo de su hermana. Y me va a disculpar mucho compadre pero para mi que la cigüeña tuvo que hacer dos viajes. ¿Sabe porqué compadre? Uno para traerlo y el otro para pedirle disculpas a los papás porque el pobre está tan, pero tan feito.
Hasta pronto compadre, aquí le voy a echar un ojo a su mamá y a sus vacas también.
Att: Su compadre Francisco

[My good friend Fernando:
Thank you for lending me the 25 pesos I asked you for, my chickens were starving. Dear friend, I hope God pays you because who knows when I could, possibly when I get my bonus. We all

miss you so much, even your cows. They have lost weight due to sadness. The only news I have is that your sister's son was born. Please forgive me for what I am going to say but the stork had to make two trips. You know why? The first one was to deliver the baby and the second one was to apologize to the parents for how ugly the baby was. Well, my dear friend, so long. I will be keeping an eye on your mother and your cows too.

Sincerely,

Your Dear Friend Francisco]

The letters reveal cultural particularity and a shared condition, the impetus for migration and the deep sense of connection to a diaspora community. At first the two characters have a conflict, but they eventually form a friendship when they realize what a difficult time they are both having in achieving the American Dream. At the end of the skit they decide to go together to a taxi dance club, where migrant workers would spend a portion of their hard-earned money paying women to dance with them. At this point in the performance, an act of fantastical revisionism takes place, past prejudices are discarded, and a modern sense of social justice and aesthetics intervenes. The characters protest their mutually exploitive condition. One character proclaims, "I don't like paying for dancing. It's not fair. We are all equal, no matter if we are farmworkers!" A contemporary Latin pop song comes over the loudspeaker, and all the children begin to dance together. One of the dancers concludes: "See how much fun we can have if we are together with no prejudice, when we are all equal!" and in Spanish, "¡*Cuando todos somos iguales!*"

WHAT THE TEACHER DIDN'T KNOW

Angelica and I received an invitation to conduct a workshop on classroom management for teachers and teacher educators. Rather than enumerate conventional strategies to reign in "off-task" children, we decided to recruit interested students from Dancing Across Borders to put together a play for the professional development opportunity. We asked the students what they would tell teachers about classroom management. When was there a productive classroom atmosphere? Why would a student adopt an oppositional stance toward school? When did school require the students to compromise or deny an aspect of who they felt they were?

The students shared stories and foraged through their writing portfolios to find samples that exemplified moments of intercultural miscommunication, conflict, and social critique. For example, Maria shared a poem in her Girl Talk journal about how she felt "invisible twice" as a Filipina, a female, and a member of an ethnic minority. Other students questioned the more punitive aspects of schooling. They eventually strung a number of these samples and vignettes together as a starting point for a script titled "What the Teacher Didn't Know," which Angelica helped shape into a dramatic performance.

In the following excerpt from "What the Teacher Didn't Know," the setting is a depressing classroom where a Dickensian schoolmaster Mr. Sid (aptly modeled after M' Choakumchild from *Hard Times*—a favorite classroom character) barks orders and reproves seemingly incorrigible youngsters. After every verbal harangue, the actors freeze as the injured party soliloquizes about the teacher's ignorance. It's important to keep in mind that the excerpts are all written by the students, including Mr. Sid's final speech.

STUDENT SUSANA: *Maestro yo, no tengo un libro para leer.*

MR. SID: Yes Susana. What? I cannot understand what you are saying?

STUDENT STEVEN: *Yo entiendo poquito espanol.* I can translate for you: She needs a book to read.

MR. SID: No! You cannot read in English, so how do you expect to read one of those blue labeled books. That table is your only choice! Everybody should get homework ready to be turned in. And this is the United States, so there will be no foreign languages!
[FREEZE]

STUDENT SUSANA: What the teacher didn't know is that I just came from Mexico five months ago, so sometimes I don't know how to say things in English. He didn't know my language is an important part of me. Speaking Spanish is something I feel proud of, but he is cruel for not encouraging me to maintain my traditions. Instead he put me down and made me feel like a stranger. And also, my teacher didn't know that people spoke Spanish here before English!

MR. SID (addressing Crystal): There is no excuse for not bringing your homework. You are a lazy, irresponsible, wretched, horrid, indolent, diminutive little beast. Don't talk to me. Go back to your seat!
[FREEZE]

STUDENT CRYSTAL: What the teacher didn't know is that I had to take care of my two little brothers and my sister. My mother worked until 8 p.m., so I was in charge of my family after school. I had to feed my brothers and change my sister's diaper. She has a disability and has difficulty caring for herself. By the time my mom got home, I was exhausted and fell asleep without having my homework done.

STUDENT MILDRED: *Kayat Ko nga mapan idyag C.R.* (I want to go to the restroom)

MR. SID: Steven can you translate that?

STUDENT STEVEN: Hey, that is not Spanish. That's Ilocano. I don't know Ilocano.

MR. SID: All those languages sound the same.

STUDENT SUSANA: *Otra vez la burra al trigo este maestro. No nos entiende.*

STUDENT FREDDY: *Tienes razón Maria. Podemos decir lo que queremos y no nos entiende.*

MR. SID: That's it! I don't like you two having a conversation that I don't understand.

STUDENT FREDDY: *Esta bien. Pero qué enojón es usted DON.*

MR. SID: What did you say?

STUDENT FREDDY: I said that you are the best teacher on the whole planet Earth.

STUDENT WILL (asleep on the teacher)

MR. SID: Will! Again, no! I cannot believe it! You are in my class-room, not in your beds. Wake up now and do what I told you.

STUDENT WILL: This class in boring and you give me a headache.

MR. SID: Well, it's your opinion! You can go out now, and find yourself a job in Taco Bell or McDonald's.
[FREEZE]

STUDENT WILL: The teacher didn't know I am on medication and that I felt robotic, lethargic, and withdrawn. Therefore I fell asleep during class because they make me take the medication in the morning. I told the teacher that I was on medication but he wouldn't listen to what I had to say. I was originally put on medication without my parents' knowledge when I lived in a group home. Medicating children can make them depend on medication for their personal problems. I am still struggling with mine. By the way, my mother is working in Taco Bell because she is struggling to feed us, and I don't see nothing wrong with that.

MR. SID: You have been reading for a while, so if I call your name please stand up and tell me about your reading. Melissa, stand up and talk to me about your reading!

STUDENT MELISSA: (quiet and afraid to talk)

MR. SID: Don't you know how to talk? Can you hear me? She looks like a robot! (everyone laughs)

MR. SID: (turns around) I guess you don't know how to talk. You know it's impolite not to answer a teacher. And look at me in the eyes when I'm speaking to you!
[FREEZE]

STUDENT MELISSA: What the teacher didn't know is that I like to be quiet because it is part of my personality and my culture. In my country women are frequently quiet because it is traditional. I did my homework and I'll like to read it to the teacher only, but not to anybody else. Also in my culture silence has meaning. It is a virtue.
[FREEZE]

MR. SID: The children don't know who I really am inside. They don't know what I have to say about them. When I tell them something, it's considered rubbish. I've lost their respect. While I was growing up, I was naive and thought that everyone should abide by what was commonly right. I guess I was wrong. Every individual has his or her own beliefs. I do too. My students come from all over the world: Mexico, China, Laos, and the Philippines. I really think it is wonderful to have a diverse classroom. When I was growing up, there wasn't much diversity. I lived with my own race. When I started teaching, I wanted to help children. Right now, I'm making these children's lives miserable. I'm just too timid and afraid to tell them who I really am. In my heart there is an opposite side. I'm really a caring and funny guy. There is just so much pressure being a teacher: raising test scores, overcrowded classes, not enough resources, struggling children. Well, this is today, and all I can do is take one day at a time.

COMMUNITY THROUGH TRANSGRESSION

Through *teatro* the students created learning experiences that slowed and expanded classroom time in order to better enable educators to focus on the perspectives, experiences, and emotions of particular children. For example, through the use of the "freezing" technique and the soliloquy in "What the Teacher Didn't Know," the daily noise of classroom interactions becomes momentarily suspended in order to foreground the students' identities. We come to understand the students as individuals whose encounters with schooling are invariably shaped by both personal and group history. When framed in this manner, their "behaviors" are not the result of traits such as *laziness* or *defiance*—almost ubiquitous accusatory categories in schools—but are rather rational responses to unjust situations.

The students' soliloquies, in fact, reveal insights derived from their unique social locations, forms of knowledge that may not be readily available to even the most well-meaning educators (university-based researchers included). This knowledge speaks to their "epistemic privilege" (Moya, 2001). The students are historically situated agents who have the capacity to reflect on their lives. Because of the dissonances of their own marginalized experiences, they are better able to explain social inequality both in their everyday lives and in the world more generally. Susana, for example, provides testimony of the relationships between language, history, and identity. Crystal articulates a class-based cultural model of childhood: the child as contributor, nurturer, and worker. Will challenges medical models for treating children who do not conform to certain expectations of how students should behave. Melissa's cultural background enables her to complicate silence as more than the mere absence of thought and meaning. And in a remarkable act of empathy, Mr. Sid's final speech discloses a form of social suffering that comes from doing an already challenging job in contexts of stark inequality without the adequate personal, material, and social resources. Taken together, the various perspectives of the characters in the drama work together to provide a complex understanding of what it may mean to teach and learn in urban schools and neighborhoods. It becomes an opportunity for diverse students to educate educators about the world and how it affects them.

The Dancing Across Borders members did in fact become publicly engaged educators. They performed their drama and dances for a variety of audiences beyond our school, including a class on Chicano/a literature and cultural studies at Stanford University, where generous college students and a committed professor provided a wonderful reception for the children and gave them a tour of the campus. The purpose of the trip to Stanford was at least twofold. The students could realize (1) that elite institutions of higher education were for them and (2) that they had invaluable perspectives to offer the university. In the current educational climate, I do not believe that goals such as these can be realized if teachers stick too closely to the mandated curriculum.

The cultural critic Ines Salazar (2000) examines African American women's and Chicana literary practice to explore how transgression may be necessary to "the enterprise of change and transformation" (p. 389). In our class, the transgressions of the *teatro* group against school norms and official ways of defining literacy and evaluation served the important function of helping to build a more inclusive classroom community. By drawing on her own passions and interests, by teaching as a Latina performance artist, Angelica created a safe space in school in which to live alternative ways of knowing and being and to ask, Why is it? Her work with the students privileged cooperation and collaborative creativity over individual achievement and competition, directed improvisation over preset objectives, ongoing group response over alienating individual assessment, and multiliteracy over monolingualism. More than anything, Angelica helped create a world that fostered joyful interdependence by putting the beautiful variations of student identity, knowledge, and expression on stage.

The Process of Inquiry

I N PART III I REFLECT ON WHAT I have learned from my students. I conceptualize a teacher research methodology that valorizes shared knowledge construction and distributes intellectual authority among members of a learning community. Chapter 8 is about one final form of school literacy practice: the stories the children reported back to me once they had moved on to middle school and high school. These ongoing stories, with traces of the worlds we once created together, should have implications for our stances as teacher researchers and are, perhaps, the ultimate arbiter of our work and its potential.

In Chapter 9 I define my own inquiry stance as a teacher researcher as an intersubjective process that is intentional, sustained, and attentive to the dialectical relationship between the students' and the teacher's own experiences and resources. I also describe the teacher researcher as an emergent professional and political identity. Finally, I describe my own literacy curriculum, which strove to be both culturally engaged and academically rigorous.

CHAPTER 8

Continuing Stories

Don't ever be afraid to start over.

—Pam Muñoz Ryan, *Esperanza Rising*

THE WRITING OF THIS BOOK has inadvertently benefited from the length of time that it took to produce and has taken on some of the characteristics of a longitudinal study. I have been able to follow the lives and learning of the children over a number of years. I have watched some of their formative school experiences unfold, and with the benefit of hindsight I draw some tentative conclusions. In this chapter I discuss the school literacy practice whereby students report back to former teachers in stories. These continuing stories, traces of the worlds we once created together with the children, have implications for our stances as teacher researchers and are, perhaps, the ultimate arbiter of our work and its potential.

The children of my class are no longer young children. They are now entering middle and high school and becoming young adults. Most have disappeared into adolescence. A number visited my classroom with regularity throughout my years in California. When I last heard from Carmen, she had taken a job helping an uncle clean a local transit station during the graveyard shift. Her grandmother was very proud that she had graduated from middle school and they were planning to move to Arizona with relatives. Carmen was looking forward to a fresh start in a new school district.

Another student, Dante, a former member of Dancing Across Borders, came to visit me for advice. He told me he had been expelled from his school for fighting and supposed gang affiliations. Dante had remembered our conversations about going to Harvard ("Where is it again, New York?") and wanted to know "what it would take to get there." Dante had what it took to get there. He was an absorbent student and an intimidating chess player. In my fifth-grade class he flew through an eighth-grade algebra textbook and had consistently scored in the 98th percentile on the mathematics portion of his standardized tests. I always felt that Stanford and Cal Tech should have had a spotlight on Dante. But along with the suspension, Dante had been kicked out of the one program in his school, a small club really, that was geared toward preparing students for college.

I also stayed in regular contact with Ada's family. Ada and her siblings also had difficulty staying in a consistent academic program. She and her family had to move from their home because a $25-a-month raise in rent was enough to make their living arrangement untenable. A month after her family moved, they had to move again because the owners of the new house decided to sell. They moved several more times before finally returning to their original home. Ada's mother explained her dilemma to me at a family barbeque. She could return to work, but that would mean leaving the children unattended. They all needed her attention, especially the eldest daughter, who was suffering severe bouts of anxiety and was afraid to go to school. Too many of the neighborhood kids, she believed, gravitated toward trouble because both parents were gone all day. So now she found herself in the uncompromising position of having to chose between providing her family with financial security or providing her children with emotional security.

One day I visited several of my former students in their new middle school. In the hour I sat in the office lobby waiting to meet with them, the police had been summoned three times to address separate conflicts. "It's like a prison here," a student casually commented as he sat by the principal's office. When I met with Ma-Lee, she informed me that things were going "pretty well," that she was getting all As and Bs, but was being "very quiet again." Her coping strategy was to keep a low profile and stay below the radar, suggesting that the journey into voice from silence in school is not linear, but situational and uneven. Maria, by contrast, was as loquacious as ever. She was rightly concerned that she may have been placed in a lower track than she deserved. This was not deliberate, but simply an oversight of a large bureaucracy; nevertheless, such an oversight can have potentially life-altering consequences for children when their parents either do not believe they can question the authority of schools or do not know how to navigate the system. Maria knew to advocate for herself. She sensed that something was amiss and recruited the help of former teachers to clarify and rectify the situation.

Celso chose to go to a neighborhood parochial school, where he, along with several other of my former students, received a full scholarship. The school adjoined the church where he had worked as an altar boy and where he was continuing as a member of a youth group. Celso's grades never took full flight, but he became close to the music teacher, the second music teacher to comment that Celso was a remarkably precocious musician. On the day of his eighth-grade graduation Celso wore a *barong*, won the music award, and was accompanied by two older students, who promised to look after him in high school.

Celso's transition to ninth grade, however, was difficult. After 3 months in a prestigious private school, attended by affluent students, on the other side of town, he returned to his local public high school. I am not sure if he ever really wanted to go to the private school; he mentioned his desire to stay with his neighborhood friends. I do know that he struggled in one of his classes because he could not afford the required text. He did not mention this to anyone because he did not want to impose himself on anyone and may have felt ashamed; in school, no one cared to ask, much less lend him a copy of the book. I thus learned that access to an elite education is not enough. Students require a supportive, nurturing environment as well as access, especially if they are crossing boundaries of class.

One message of the children's stories is that our educational system is fragile at best. Gains in test scores may provide a sense of comfort and control for educators, but they should not draw attention away from the immediacy of actual student lives that are affected by the vicissitudes of poverty and the unexpected contingencies of a large, underresourced school district. I believe that many students were to varying degrees conscious of their educational predicaments—as I was—but consciousness was not always enough to significantly alter their educational trajectories.

What then does it mean to teach in such uncertain conditions? In my view, teachers need to adopt a Janusian approach, to have their work informed by two apparently contradictory stances. The first stance is to never imagine our students as not succeeding, to sustain an unconditional faith in each student. Vivian Gadsden reminds teachers of the importance of teaching every child with the expectation that they will surpass the teachers' own accomplishments. My father reminded me to never discount any child, to remember my grandfather, where he was from and what he had survived. In schools, this faith requires working both within and against dominant curricular practices. We teach students to do well on their high-stakes tests while agitating to get rid of the tests. We advocate for students to be placed in the college track while supporting thoughtful reforms to abolish tracking. And we provide a rigorous (inter)disciplinary knowledge base while creating learning engagements that address the specificities of the students' experiences, histories, social identities, and needs. Perhaps most important teachers require an inexhaustible believing stance toward their students. If there is a setback, every new day is an opportunity to start over. I think that at times the romantic tone of this book is a form of resistance, a way for me to counterbalance the often bleak and deterministic discourses surrounding urban education and urban students.

With this believing stance toward students, teachers must adopt a more skeptical stance toward dominant explanations of student failure, such as the notion of talent and ability, or the subtle and not so subtle insinuations of cultural or class superiority. They also need to work against the inertia and spectacular injustice of the system. Statistically speaking, schools do in fact fail many urban students. But I did not need statistics to be convinced of this. The students' own stories reveal the social, not the personal, origins of student failure. That is, the concrete realities of social inequality produce failure. An obligation to these realities should prompt teachers to think of their roles more expansively and attend to *extracurricular* responsibilities beyond the walls of the school. Teachers are in a unique position to understand what schools need and to suggest to wider audiences that an equitable distribution of resources should be thought of as a precondition—not a reward—for educational progress. Part of becoming a more literate teacher involves becoming an educational activist.

For example, during my last years at the school were a number of important developments in the neighborhood. The church youth group took an active interest in cultural heritage. Individuals who had grown up in the area and had gone off for advanced degrees in subjects such as history and Asian American studies were now returning to educate and inspire younger generations. And perhaps most notable, an intergenerational and multiethnic coalition of academics, citizens, and youth were in the process of protecting and revitalizing a historically Filipino part of the neighborhood that was designated as a national historic site. In the process they were reclaiming a group history while addressing current community needs. One of my lost opportunities as a teacher was not to more proactively tap into these ongoing legacies of local organization and activism.

But a number of the children would tap into these community resources on their own. For example, Priscilla became very involved in these and other community activities. The last letter I received from her indicated that she was creating for herself an empowering school identity that was consonant with her personal and cultural identity: "I play basketball for the high school. I also participate on the Badminton Club, Red Cross, and Key Club. As for my academics, I am currently, and always will be, enrolled in Honors classes."

I have also recently heard from Leticia. She was still both a scholar and an activist in high school. She had exemplary academic achievement, with her sights firmly set on college. Leticia and her family were also deeply involved in the immigrant rights movement.

Jasmine was another student whom many people wrote off at an early age. The last I heard from her, she was about to enter ninth grade. As she grew older, her vision of possibility widened in proportion to her expanding web of support. She had always had a grandmother who believed in her. She was in a church choir; had roots in her family's Baptist church; developed a social life around the local YMCA; and has recruited a number of advocates, including school- and university-based educators. Jasmine handed me the following letter from her counselor:

TO WHOM IT MAY CONCERN:

Today I tested Jasmine's progress in reading, spelling, and arithmetic. She did exceptionally well. She is reading at the college level and spelling at 12th grade. Her math skills are about 10th-grade level. This is an outstanding achievement for Jasmine. She has applied herself to learning and is very successful. You can be proud of her efforts. She has the potential to meet her goals and fulfill her dreams.

Normally suspicious about standardized tests and fixed grade-level designations, I accepted these results. I told Jasmine I was happy that others were beginning to realize what we had known since fifth grade.

CHAPTER 9

Systematic Improvisation

A Way of Teaching and Researching

M Y RESEARCH METHOD HAS DEVELOPED out of my day-to-day work as a teacher researcher in an urban, multiethnic neighborhood elementary school in California. It is an organic model in the sense that my design intention, data collection, and means of interpretation were not formulated a priori and then applied to my practice; rather, full immersion in the multiple and interacting currents of the life-stream of the classroom was the first in a series of moves intended to generate knowledge-of-practice. Each move, in turn, spawned new stories, interpretations, and classroom actions. The inquiry produced its own logic, which I call *systematic improvisation*.

The method is improvisational because it acknowledges that the students possess valuable and relevant knowledge to bring to bear on their educational development. This suggests that my ability to effectively teach the children is predicated on my ability to learn from them. Learning from the students involves remaining open and willing to incorporate their ever-evolving experiences into the class, however unpredictable or at odds with the school's agenda or my own preconceptions. The dialectical process is roughly sketched like this: As the teacher, I enter the classroom with my own background and intentions, including the pragmatic and urgent concern to allow the students to seize on their own capacities for critical reflection that enable them to negotiate fruitfully the demands of the school. The students, in turn, encounter the class with their own cultural resources, interests, values, and cares. It is the cross-pollination of these two sets of experiences that fuels the inquiry, in that I continually modify my understanding of the class in light of my interactions with the students and ideally they arrive at a greater realization of their own academic potential based on membership in the classroom community.

In this sense, our collaborative inquiry was a form of ongoing meaning making and an act of professional survival, a way to respond to the complexities and uncertainties of working, learning, and living in urban neighborhoods and schools. This is not to suggest that there was always progress. But adapting an inquiry stance into my work did entail a sustained commitment to exploring moments of dissonance and frustration as opportunities for professional growth.

COMMITMENT TO INQUIRY

Given the amount of work involved in urban teaching, such a commitment to inquiry may only gain traction if it is deliberately and systematically manifested in some form that is intrinsic to the daily operations of the class. This means that our methodology, methods, and classroom practices are inextricably connected. In this study, both the form and the mode of inquiry was the ethnic/migrant narrative, which I employed to mediate and illuminate the generative nexus between the students' and the teachers' own interests and resources. I define the ethnic/migrant narrative as a story one tells to explain and gain some degree of control over one's experiences crossing social and political boundaries and borders. These stories often thematize geographic dislocation, movement, and transcultural interaction in contexts in which issues of power cannot be ignored. This admittedly liberal definition allows a wide range of the students' school literacy practices, such as their autobiographies, prose, poetry, oral conversations, interviews, scripts, and performances, all of which serve as sources for this study. It is also flexible enough to take into account the experiences of those students who are not technically defined as migrants by institutional criteria, for example, children whose movements between geographic regions, towns, homes, schools, and even classrooms entail profound social disjuncture that may typically go unnoticed. The category of ethnic/migrant narrative, however, also includes the chapters of this book itself, which are in some ways an extension and translation for an academic audience of the children's stories as well as reflections on my own family's immigrant history and how it has informed my stance as an urban teacher researcher.

It is important to emphasize that the writing of the chapters was very much part of the inquiry process. It was recursive and self-generating. Each chapter planted the seeds for the one that followed and was inseparable from the process of formulating new learning experiences with the students.

I did not first gather, then categorize, and finally explicate my data in a linear fashion. Instead, I engaged in an ongoing struggle to create a coherent and more empowering narrative of teaching and learning. For example, I would not have known that children would use autobiography to work through trauma had I not taken a critical look at the ways in which the established curriculum excluded the very experiences I invited them to explore. It was only afterward, when they were able to begin communicating what they had endured or lost, could I fully apprehend the importance that school literacy might play in allowing the children to orient themselves in diaspora communities. Literacy became one means of recuperating cultural competencies, traditions, and residual cultural values that would enable students to adapt to and succeed in school. And finally the students' performances with the *teatro* group Dancing Across Borders drew on their previous work. It would have been unimaginable were it not for the accretive and cumulative process of inquiry that had been done up to that point. The students' narrative performances describing their achievement of more fully realized ethnic identities proved to be coextensive and integral to their academic success and my own process of generating knowledge-of-practice.

Each new phase of the inquiry required me to forage for new resources (both indirect classroom resources—academic or otherwise—that helped me conceptualize the students' work and materials that the children engaged directly to generate new texts) and discover new patterns of meaning and relevance and prompted new collaborative investigations. One implication for teacher research is that it may not be possible to postulate the entire body of literature that is pertinent to study before the research has begun. The appropriate literature sources emerge out of the inquiry process. A corollary point is that because it is an ongoing process, there may not be definite boundaries to teacher research, no clear beginning and end. In more conventional research terms, teacher research has built within it an internal dynamic feedback mechanism. It is this feedback mechanism that prompts us to continually refine our practices and interpretive frameworks.

The narratives I share are therefore both a catalyst and a product of the inquiry process. There were, in fact, many possible stories, as the children collectively generated a rich and compelling array of narratives. I chose to focus on certain individuals because they provide representative examples. The works of Celso, Ma-Lee, Carmen, Priscilla, and Maria are emblematic of the ways in which many of the students used memory, storytelling, *teatro*, and family history as sites for autobiographical writing and engagement with and reading of their worlds. I also believe that several of the students recruited me. The very act of teacher research itself often fortifies social bonds, and some of the children may have found participation in the process useful at that point in their lives.

THE TEACHER RESEARCHER AS AN EMERGENT
PROFESSIONAL AND ACTIVIST IDENTITY

My experiences have convinced me that teachers must be more than institutional functionaries divorced from the experiences of their students. They might instead self-consciously cultivate membership in the community. I propose thinking about the urban teacher researcher as an emergent and more fully integrated social identity. By *emergent* I mean that this identity is already forming but needs to be named and then encouraged in a self-conscious and systematic way.

This involves stretching the ideas of *social location* and *inquiry stance*. It stretches *social location* to include our professional and ideological affiliations, suggesting that our daily work in urban schools may provide a unique vantage point from which to study education. It also requires thinking about how our individual inquiries contribute to a collective knowledge base. As urban teacher researchers *collaboratively* inquire into their own practices in a wide variety of settings *over time*, they may begin to notice salient patterns, recurrent themes, similar concerns, and observations that resemble one another and that, when conceptualized together, begin to have explanatory power and general relevance. Despite the differences in teaching contexts and between researchers, these features may point to aspects of a shared phenomenology. Teacher researchers' experiences, taken as a whole, may begin to constitute a type of social identity.

What, then, are the experiential features that characterize this emergent identity and influence the ways in which teacher research is constructed and represented? How specifically might it differ from more conventional research paradigms? I will take stock of some of the features of this identity under the following interrelated headings: the teacher researcher as (1) an interested, (2) a vulnerable, and (3) a relational social identity. These are not new ideas, but I believe they are worth reiterating as vital ideas for teacher researchers as we attempt to stake out our own ground both in our own school sites and in the academy.

The Teacher Researcher as an Interested Identity

As teacher researchers we may recognize that our scholarship is inherently political and interested. We are interested in defamiliarizing schooling in order to (re)familiarize ourselves with our students: with their histories, values, and traditions and, ultimately, their fully realized potential and humanity. These two processes occur in tandem and are inextricable. We remain interested because we experience the consequences of our work with an immediacy and poignancy. There is a physical, material component to teaching, an emotional and bodily strenuousness. There is no separation between contemplation and "menial" labor, between intellectual inquiry and social responsibility. We are literally on the ground with our students, spending countless hours planning, completing paperwork, organizing our rooms, sitting in meetings, performing for evaluators, attending to emotional needs, comforting children with asthma, visiting homes, participating in community events, administering tests, and responding to children's work long into the night. These are daily facts.

Sometimes we are resolving conflicts, breaking up fights, protesting misguided policies, spending hours in the office trying not to have a child suspended or tracked. After the bell rings, we meet with former students trying to figure out what happened, why they are so disaffected when once so excited about school. We continue to advise students who have gone on to college, or ones who have found themselves in the criminal justice system. We pay our respects at funerals and try our best to counsel children about death and loss. In one year, three of my students' caretakers passed away from poverty-related causes. These realities of the heart and body are inherent in the nature of our inquiries and the very material from which we theorize our practice and shape our political stance.

Sometimes our resistance takes an overt political form and is aligned with larger activist movements. Other times, it is more subtle but is resistance nonetheless; for example, our efforts to expand time and open up opportunities for reflection, creativity, and bonding with our students may radically interrupt the institutional drive for efficiency and standardization.

One of the most urgent challenges for urban teacher researchers may be to reformulate a progressive language that has political efficacy because it is grounded in the actual lives of children and is persuasive about what is required for urban students to flourish. We need to communicate the complexity of our work with pragmatic effects.

The Teacher Researcher as a Vulnerable Identity

One of the more potent aspects of my teaching has involved almost daily thoughts that I might be doing a disservice to a student, that an action or decision might be based on a misreading of a social situation, a dearth of contextual information, or my own lack or awareness. When there is a change in an individual child's mood, when he or she becomes more reticent or withdrawn, more distant or resistant, when the atmosphere in the class shifts in a negative direction, I worry that my actions may have caused or exacerbated a delicate situation. While these thoughts may become intrusive, they may also be thought of more productively as opportunities for professional growth.

Inquiry as a *stance*, as a type of spatial orientation, involves resisting the stifling urge to categorize in order to make room for the individual children themselves to more fully develop and articulate their own experiences so we can question our own, ingrained assumptions.

Following Ruth Behar (1996), I have chosen the word *vulnerable* to highlight the affective component our work and the acute realization of just how fallible we are when teaching and learning across cultural boundaries. When it comes to "knowing" children, a little humility is in order. Too often in urban schools, "knowing" children has involved reducing them to numbers and assimilating their experiences into prescribed curricula or even our own preconceptions. Part of being vulnerable involves an admission that any attempt at certainty may invariably involve some form of exclusion. In our school sites, we may be wary of overly authoritative claims, such as the idea of best practices that are transferable across contexts or that there is one way to teach children. There is always something unfinished about our investigations. Vulnerability becomes a type of reflexive disposition that keeps us vigilant about lapsing into comfortable professional roles (of certified so-called specialist, expert, master, or scholar) that may obscure our own partiality and the continued need to expand our understanding through others.

The Teacher Researcher as a Relational Identity

Our attempts at building relationships—with students and families, with colleagues, across cultural, institutional and disciplinary boundaries—have epistemic significance because it is a way in which we both socially and cognitively contextualize our work. I am intentionally stepping back from the nominalization of the word *context* to emphasize both process and the constant attention we place on nurturing our total classroom environment. For much of conventional educational research, context is a static entity (often relegated to one section in a monograph or paper) and the researcher an observer of the context who employs methods to focus on something discrete. As teacher researchers, we recognize how we are implicated in actively shaping the various, at times conflicting contexts in our professional lives.

This means we are always trying to relate any portion of our research to the whole of our work. We may focus on a specific pedagogical situation or event, but only if it crystallizes or contributes to a larger dynamic or is related to an understanding of our students as complete human beings. There is an improvisational component to teacher inquiry, where we have background knowledge and a plan, but we must also respond creatively and thoughtfully to the contingencies of the classroom. This type of pedagogy of improvisation may, in fact, take more preparation than either a research methodology or an instructional approach, in which each step in the process is clearly delineated and sequenced beforehand.

As teachers we should assert our unqualified membership in a vibrant and emergent intellectual—and, hopefully, activist—culture. I believe it would be part of the work that, as Sonia Nieto (2003) put it, "keeps teachers going." Perhaps more than anything, this involves envisioning and working toward more just social and educational arrangements by affirming the very experiences that brought us to inquiry in the first place, those of our students.

OUR LITERACY CURRICULUM

During initial presentations of my research with fifth graders, a number of people commented on the sophistication of the children's writing. They often wanted to know what was done to facilitate such impressive work. As in many classrooms, our literacy curriculum was driven by an intensive commitment to the intertwined and collaborative processes of reading, writing, storytelling, sharing, and reflection.

Our classroom also benefited from a rich tradition of educational research that recognizes the holistic nature of teaching and learning and conceptualizes a wide array of student-centered strategies to generate powerful learning experiences. Adopting an inquiry stance does not exclude these strategies; quite the opposite, it situates them within a purposeful and deliberative context. I have intentionally bracketed or only alluded to these approaches because this study is not meant to be comprehensive or prescriptive. No one strategy, or even combination of strategies, led to the children's stories and essays.

I offer just a rough sketch of an average day to signal how immersed the students were in school literacy. In the morning we would begin with one of a number of ritual classroom greetings. These took the form of poems, call-and-response chants, or a reminder to the students that they were their parents' and grandparents' "walking and talking dreams." I would also have the children point to their "diamonds" (their brains) and to their "rubies" (their hearts). We then would share a "letter of the day," addressed to the whole class (at first written by myself, then taken over by the students), which would recognize, on a rotating basis, the accomplishments of individual children. The letters included a list of "workshop items," which involved both mandatory curricula and individualized projects. The students would continue workshop all day while breaking up into smaller learning groups. These groups were heterogeneous, porous, and often facilitated by the students themselves. Among such groups were Girl Talk; Pinoy Teach, which drew from the Pinoy Teach curriculum by Cordova and Espiritu (2001); and the Dancing Across Borders *teatro* ensemble. Many were organized around books and given shape by our collaborative inquiries into immigration or multiculturalism.

The students did an intensive amount of reading, writing, and reflective speaking. They interacted with a variety of young adult fiction, including popular novels by Lois Lowry, Francisco Jimenez, Mildred Taylor, Jerry Spinelli, Pam Munoz Ryan, Louis Sacher, and many others. They also read canonical works such as *Heidi, Little Women, The Chronicles of Narnia*, Tolkien's *Rings* trilogy, Greek mythology, and traditional folktales from around the world. At times I would select passages from authors such as Esmeralda Santiago, Carlos Bulosan, and Sandra Cisneros, and the poetry of Shakespeare, William Blake, Langston Hughes, Rudolfo Anaya, and June Jordan. The children also shared family letters, song lyrics, magazine articles, and community *dichos* (wise sayings). Most of the students read at least twelve novels throughout the year, in addition to a substantial amount of nonfiction.

There were other aspects of my pedagogy, which were a bit more explicit and directed. In addition to having the students absorb an immense amount of print, I also stressed vocabulary through daily cloze activities, personal dictionaries, and informal classroom discourse. The students learned at least 30 new words a week, which they culled from the various texts they were reading. These big, "10-dollar" words, as the students called them, would eventually seep into their own writing and become a valuable resource for them to name and articulate their experiences. I would also teach "minilessons" to smaller groups of children who needed reinforcement of particular academic conventions. It was my aim to provide significant instructional time to the students beyond the regular school hours. I was fortunate to have many adults, including student teachers and parents, volunteer to give children more personalized attention. In fact I had an open-door policy for any committed and talented person willing to get busy and work.

Toward the end of my first year I had established myself as a teacher and was given more flexibility with the curriculum. This enabled the class to spend time on events such as poetry readings and drama. I could also customize curricula for individual children, especially those more resistant to traditional schooling. I discovered how reading, writing, and researching about issues relevant to one's immediate life could in fact become a cultural release for oppositional impulses.

During my second year, my reputation was reinforced by the students' gains on their standardized-test scores in language arts and mathematical skills, which increased on average between 10 and 15 percentile points in each category. Furthermore, over the following 2 years, the gains were more substantial. While I always believed that the students could perform well on a variety of measures if we followed an inquiry approach, they in fact did much better than I had expected achieving greater increases in their scores than did students in classrooms in the district where test preparation and remediation were the primary focus.

In my view, the most important ingredient in the students' powerful narratives was the relationships they forged through inquiry, which is ultimately about the creative alchemy of a particular community of learners. What I have called the "second classroom"—the spaces and interactions created with the students before school, after school, during recess, at neighborhood and community events, and eventually during regular hours—played an instrumental role in helping to sustain these relationships. In this book I have tried to capture something of the essence of our relational knowledge production.

References

Alcoff, L., & Mohanty, S. (2006). Reconsidering identity politics: An introduction. In L. Alcoff, M. Hames-Garcia, S. Mohanty, and P. Moya (Eds.), *Identity politics reconsidered*. New York: Palgrave Macmillan.

Anzaldúa, G. (1987). *Borderlands/La frontera: The new mestiza*. San Francisco: Spinsters/Aunt Lute.

Behar, R. (1996). *The vulnerable observer*. Boston: Beacon Press.

Bohulano Mabalon, D. (2005). Bomber pilots and basketball players: Second-generation Filipina Americans in Stockton, California, 1930s to 1950s. In M. de Jesus (Ed.), *Pinay power: Theorizing the Filipina/American experience* (pp. 117–133). New York: Routledge.

Bourdieu, P. (Ed.). (1993). *The weight of the world: Social suffering in contemporary society*. Stanford: Stanford University Press.

Boym, S. (2001). *The future of nostalgia*. New York: Basic Books.

Broyles-González, Y. (1994). *El Teatro Campesino*. Austin: University of Texas Press.

Bulosan, C. (1973). *America is in the heart*. Seattle: University of Washington Press. (Original work published 1946)

Carini, P. (2001). *Starting strong*. New York: Teachers College Press.

Carter, S. (2001). *The possibilities of silence: Adolescent African-American female cultural identity in secondary English classrooms*. Unpublished doctoral dissertation, Vanderbilt University.

Caruth, C. (1996). *Unclaimed experience: Trauma, narrative, and history*. Baltimore: Johns Hopkins University Press.

Cheung, K.-K. (1993). *Articulate silences*. Ithaca: Cornell University Press.

Cisneros, S. (1987). *House on Mango Street*. New York: Vintage.

Clifford, J. (1997). *Routes: Travel and translation in the late twentieth century*. Cambridge, MA: Harvard University Press.

Cochran-Smith, M., & Lytle, S. L. (1999). Relationships of knowledge and practice: Teacher learning in communities. In A. Iran-Nejad & P. D. Pearson (Eds.), *Review of research in education* (pp. 249–305). Washington, DC: American Educational Research Association.

Cochran-Smith, M., & Lytle, S. L. (2001). Beyond certainty: Taking an inquiry stance on practice. In A. M. Lieberman (Ed.), *Teachers caught in the action: Professional development that matters* (pp. 46–60). New York: Teachers College Press.

Cordova, T., & Espiritu, P. C. (2001). *Pinoy Teach: A multicultural curriculum exploring Filipino history and culture* (4th ed.). Seattle: Filipino Youth Activities.

Edmiston, B. (2000). Drama as ethical education. *Research in Drama Education, 5*(1), 63–84.

Fairclough, N. (2000). *New labour, new language?* London: Routledge.

Fecho, B. (2003). *Is this English? Race, language, and culture in the classroom.* New York: Teachers College Press.

Freire, P. (1996). *Pedagogy of the oppressed.* (M. Bergman Ramos, Trans.). New York: Continuum (Original work published 1970)

Freire, P. (1998). *Teachers as cultural workers: Letters to those who dare to teach.* (D. Macedo, D. Koike, & A. Oliveira, Trans.) Boulder, CO: Westview Press. (Original work published 1993)

Gadsden, V. (1992). Giving meaning to literacy: Intergenerational beliefs about access. *Theory into Practice, 31*, 328–335.

Gonzalez, N., Moll, L., Tenery, M., Rivera, A., Rendon, P., Gonzales, R., & Amanti, C. (1995). Funds of knowledge for teaching in Latino households. *Urban Education, 29*, 443–470.

Greene, M. (1994). Multiculturalism, community, and the arts. In A. Hass Dyson & C. Genishi (Eds.), *The need for story* (pp. 11–27). Urbana, IL: National Council of Teachers of English.

Gutierrez, G. (1995). *Sharing the Word through the liturgical year.* New York: Maryknoll.

Gutierrez, K., Barquedano-Lopez, P., & Tejeda, C. (1999). Rethinking diversity: Hybridity and hybrid language practices in the third space. *Mind, Culture, and Activity, 6*, 286–303.

Gutierrez, K., Barquedano-Lopez, P., & Turner, M. G. (1999). Building a culture of collaboration through hybrid language practices. *Theory into Practice, 38*(2), 87-93.

Hesford, W. (1999). *Framing identities: Autobiography and the politics of pedagogy.* Minneapolis: University of Minnesota Press.

Hochschild, A. R. (2000). Global care chains and emotional surplus value. In W. Hutton & A. Giddens (Eds.), *Global capitalism* (pp. 130–146). New York: New Press.

Hughes, L. (1994). *Collected poems.* New York: Knopf.

Jordan, J. (1995). *June Jordan's poetry for the people.* New York: Routledge.

Latina Feminist Group (2001). Introduction: Papelitos guardados: Theorizing Latinidades through testimonio. In The Latina Feminist Group (Ed.), *Telling to live: Latina feminist testimonios* (pp. 1–24). Durham: Duke University Press.

Levinson, B., Foley, D., & Holland, D. (1996). *The cultural production of the education person.* Albany: State University of New York Press.

Lowe, L. (1996). *Immigrant acts.* Durham: Duke University Press.

Lytle, S. L. (1993). Risky business. *The Quarterly, 15*(1), 20–32.

Medina, C. (2004). Drama wor(l)ds: Explorations of Latina/o realistic fiction through drama. *Language Arts, 81*, 272–282.

Mehan, H. (1996). The construction of an LD student. In M. Silverstein & G. Urban (Eds.), *Natural histories of discourse* (pp. 253–276). Chicago: University of Chicago Press.

Mendoza Strobel, L. (2000). "Born-again Filipino": Filipino American identity and panethnicity. In A. Singh & P. Schmidt (Eds.), *Postcolonial theory and the United States* (pp. 349–369). Jackson: University of Mississippi.

Mohanty, S. (1997). *Literary theory and the claims of history: Postmodernism, objectivity, multicultural politics.* Ithaca: Cornell University Press.

Moya, P. (2000). Postmodernism, "realism," and the politics of identity. In P. Moya & M. Hames-Garcia (Eds.), *Reclaiming identity: Realist theory and the predicament of postmodernism* (pp. 67–101). Berkeley: University of California Press.

Moya, P. (2001). *Learning from experience: Minority identities, multicultural struggles.* Berkeley: University of California Press.

Moya, P., & Hames-Garcia, M. (Eds.). (2000). *Reclaiming identity: Realist theory and the predicament of postmodernism.* Berkeley: University of California Press.

Muñoz Ryan, P. *Esperanza rising.* New York: Scholastic.

Nieto, S. (1996). *Affirming diversity.* New York: Addison Wesley Longman.

Nieto, S. (2003). *What keeps teachers going?* New York: Teachers College Press.

Nussbaum, M. C. (1996). Reply. In M. C. Nussbaum (Ed.), *For love of country: Debating the limits of patriotism* (pp. 131–144). Boston: Beacon Press.

Ogbu, J., & Simons, H. D. (1998). Voluntary and involuntary minorities: A cultural-ecological theory of school performance with some implications for education. *Anthropology and Education Quarterly, 29*(2), 155–188.

Pincus, M. (2005). Learning from Laramie: Urban high school students read, research, and reenact *The Laramie Project.* In T. Hatch, D. Ahmed, A. Lieberman, D. Faigenbaum, M. White, & D. Pointer Mace (Eds.), *Going public with our teaching.* New York: Teachers College Press.

Quartz, K. H., Olsen, B., & Duncan-Andrade, J. (2004). *The fragility of urban teaching: A longitudinal study of career development and activism.* Los Angeles: Institute for Democracy, Education, and Access, UCLA.

Rosaldo, R. (1989). *Culture and truth.* Boston: Beacon Press.

Rushdie, S. (1980). *Midnight's children.* New York: Penguin Books.

Rushdie, S. (1991). *Haroun and the Sea of Stories.* New York: Viking & Granta.

Salazar, I. (2000). Can you go home again? Transgression and transformation in African-American women's and Chicana literary practice. In A. Singh & P. Schmidt (Eds.), *Postcolonial theory* (pp. 388–411). Jackson: University Press of Mississippi.

Scarry, E. (1996). The difficulty of imagining other people. In M. C. Nussbaum (Ed.), *For love of country: Debating the limits of patriotism* (pp. 98–110). Boston: Beacon Press.

Shultz, K. (2003). *Listening: A framework for teaching across differences.* New York: Teachers College Press.

Sollors, W. (1990). Ethnicity. In F. Lentricchia & T. McLaughlin (Eds.), *Critical terms for literary study* (pp. 288–306). Chicago: University of Chicago Press.

Street, B. V. (1984). *Literacy in theory and practice.* Cambridge: Cambridge University Press.

Street, B. V. (Ed.). (1993). *Cross-cultural approaches to literacy.* Cambridge: Cambridge University Press.

Street, B. V. (Ed.). (2001). *Literacy and development.* London: Routledge.

Waff, D. (1994). Girl Talk: Creating community through social exchange. In M. Fine (Ed.), *Chartering urban school reform: Reflections of a public high school in the midst of change.* New York: Teachers College Press.

Walcott, D. (1998). *What the twilight says.* New York: Farrar, Straus, & Giroux.

Wolf, S., & Enciso, P. (1994). Multiple selves in literary interpretation: Engagement and the language of drama. In C. Kinzer & D. Lieu (Eds.), *Multidimensional aspects of literacy research, theory, and practice* (pp. 351–360). Chicago: National Reading Conference.

Zamora, L. P., & Faris, W. B. (Eds.). (1995). *Magical realism: Theory, history, community.* Durham: Duke University Press.

Index

About the Author

Gerald Campano is currently an assistant professor of education at Indiana University, Bloomington. Before that, he taught school for nine years, served in Teach for America, and was a Carnegie Scholar. He has been nominated as "Teacher of the Year" in several schools.